Investment Worthy Startup

H. TOMI DAVIES

WOW Book Publishing™

Dedication

This book is dedicated to those aspiring and using innovation to build a better Africa and my two grandsons Kayinoluwa and Kayokari whom I hope get to read this book in the future. I've put all I know about building great African startup companies in here for you to use and make even better. All my love. - **Gramps (TD)**

Contents

Investment Worthy Startup

...building business ventures investors want to fund

By H. Tomi Davies

Synopsis

This is a book that helps startup founders and their investors have a conversation about how best to build a successful startup. What this book will hopefully do is give you as startup founders the framework to manage this process. It focuses on your startup journey, from start to - well... does it have an end?

A startup vision can be brought to life using the POEM Framework®. This acronym stands for Proposition, Organisation, Economics and Milestones. In this book, I share how you use the POEM Framework® to successfully build a startup business venture.

First things first, the book defines what a startup is and what it's not with innovation at the heart of everything a startup is and the genesis of its definition. Startups are innovative commercial ventures built for rapid and even explosive growth. This means they are continuously in need of capital which makes their funding profile different to that of small and medium-sized business enterprises (SMEs) even though they typically start as one.

Let me borrow the metaphor of a train journey to explain the startup journey and measuring progress along the way which the book explains.

At the beginning of the journey, the startup founders use their own money to get the business off the ground, usually with financial support from family, friends, fans and fools - the FFF, or what I like to call the FFFFF funding stage. This is pretty much the train getting ready to leave the station for its mission-driven destination.

The departure point is a minimum viable product (MVP) which brings in the first customers and the Angel round of funding to keep the customers coming, build a better product and get more people on board. With the train in full motion, we start to see revenue growth as the startup gains traction which triggers the first early-stage Venture Capital (VC) funding round which is the pre-seed round.

At this point, you as the startup founders are on top of what's happening in your startups market, who your customers are, who's on your team, the tech you have, how many lives your startup has touched, how much capital you have and how quickly you're burning it.

With all this information now at your disposal on the upside, your startup can now attract later-stage VC investors (or even potential buyers) funding your seed round to fully establish your product market fit (PMF).

And the journey goes on with you as the founders aim to double revenues each year as your startup venture grows and hopefully becomes more successful.

To press all the levers needed to progress through the different stages, founders will need to understand exactly what they need, whom they need it from, how soon, in what measure, and perhaps quite crucially how long they have before they get to the next stage or stop.

So back on the train metaphor and you're looking at a dashboard which lets you know you have two minutes to the next stop, about twenty minutes to the one after, and an hour to the fifth stop from the next one. You don't just see the immediate revenue or customer targets in front of you, but you know what you need to do before you get to the tenth stop which could be Series A, B or C.

That's where the POEM Framework® comes in. It enables you as founders to see what is needed many stops down the line while working to meet your startups immediate-term needs.

Over the years my family and friends always said to me; "you have a really simple way of explaining these things so why not put it into a book". So, while there are quite a number of extremely useful books out there on and about startups, some of which I have learnt a tremendous lot from, one thing I think some could change, is making the language simpler.

Just because you have an amazing idea that could become a great startup does not mean that you're au fait with all the technical terms used in the fast-growing startup and business investment world. I trust this book helps.

Foreword

Dear Reader

The Investment Worthy Startup is the book you need to read if you want to learn how you build a viable startup company in Africa that can attract funding from Angel investors and Venture Capital firms.

TD has had some unique experiences and gathered a lot of knowledge about startups in Africa which he imparts to you in a way that enables understanding, insights and most importantly application.

The knowledge in his book has the power to help you build the startup you need in a way that it gets funded by those who bet on startups. I can tell you as a seasoned founder and Angel investor who has written books on this topic, that TD provides a guide that will no doubt empower any founder building a startup venture on the African continent and elsewhere.

I can also tell you from my 30+ years of experience in the startup world that TD brings to the table a wealth of experience, expertise, skills, and capabilities to help you build the right startup of your dreams and get it funded properly.

Enjoy the read.

- David S Rose
Award-winning Author and International Speaker
David founded, and is Chairman Emeritus of,
New York Angels, one of the world's largest
and most active angel investment groups.

Testimonials

"Don't build your startup in Africa or invest in one without reading this book."

\- Gerrad Olisa-Ashar,
Cybersecurity Expert, Oxford, UK

"TD's electric charisma and extensive network helped us get off the mark in Nigeria with significant momentum. He is a thoughtful collaborator and a valuable partner for founders embarking on their entrepreneurship journey."

\- Dr Ashifi Gogo, Founder/CEO, Sproxil Inc.

"In 2017, I started Powerstove without knowing what the future holds except proving the concept that a stove can be clean and generate electricity. That was the goal. Vision didn't go beyond the euphoria of a tech breakthrough until by happenstance I stumbled across an Angel in South Africa. Tomi Davies is that Angel that believed in the future of the inventor more than the technology. He saw more in me than I could and went all out to keep sacrificing his resources, time and network to support Powerstove from MVP to Sustainable Scaling Business."

- Okey Esse, Founder/CEO, Powerstove

"TD is doing wonderful things by sharing his experience & knowledge with me and other Techpreneurs. I'm forever grateful for his guidance and advice."

- Yusuf Badmos

"Techpreneurs interested in being mentored by TD can expect intelligent dialogues that will influence you to be a better person and in turn create tangible value to your society."

- Damilola Ademilokun

"In 2017, I met TD in Istanbul during the StartupIstanbul event where FlexiSAF pitched about their edtech solution and how they help schools improve their processes and ROI using software. In just a few minutes of chatting with TD, I was amazed at his depth of experience and passion to support startups. I was fortunate to pitch live to the audience while TD watched. I recall what he told me when we next met, "I am going to help you grow and raise funds." 4 years later, as an investor and advisory board member, TD has supported FlexiSAF to scale and sustain the business. He is instrumental in our strategy, corporate governance, networking, and business development. TD is the number 1 Angel investor I know in Africa and does it passionately."

- Faiz Bashir, Co-Founder/CEO, FlexiSAF

"TD challenged me to be a better version of myself. I challenged my preconceived boundaries and limiting beliefs and achieved more than I thought I would."

- Seun Abimbola

"TD is adept at unravelling the secrets of failing startups and focusing them towards traction"

- Ola Oyo

"I have known TD for over 10 years. While many will only support you when you are succeeding , TD has been there encouraging me in success and failure alike. He is a huge influence in my personal and business Journey."

- Deepankar Rustagi, Founder/CEO, Omnibiz

"His mentorship programme has enabled me to learn a lot from TD's experiences and those within the group. I have adopted key traits for business success, and now place major importance on focus."

- Funmilayo Amarvi

"Tomi Davies has been a supporter, investor and board member in Big Cabal Media since I first joined the company. He's been an invaluable resource in fundraising, pragmatic problem solving and a source of advice when the going got tough. TD has an excellent and wide-ranging network that greatly respects him, and he is more than willing to put that network to use in service of his portfolio companies and the many startups that he supports."

- Tomiwa Aladekomo,
CEO, Big Cabal Media

"TD's book provides a road map for building startups that get funded in Africa"

- Stephen Ozoigbo,
Tech Executive, Silicon Valley, California

"TD pours his years of experience working with African startups into this book making it worth reading"

- Aly El Shalakany,
Lawyer, Cairo Egypt

Acknowledgements

I acknowledge the souls of the dearly departed who have inspired my earth's journey including Jesus Christ my Lord, my late father Hezekiah Oladipo Davies (HOD) and grandfather Benjamin Feyisayo Oluwole (Big Ben), Max Erhman for Desiderata and Rudyard Kipling for IF.

I'd like to thank Tom Watson, Vinton Cerf, Bill Gates, Gordon Bell, Livinus Ike Onunaku, Alan Kaye, Bob Lucky, Steve Jobs, Larry Ellison, Philip Emeagwali, Tim Berners-Lee, Mark Zuckerberg, Larry Page & Jerry Yang, Jeff Bezos, and many others whom I've not named but who have helped to make this world a better place for you and me through our use of technology as humans.

I acknowledge some of the great minds that I've had the pleasure of learning from and also being associated with including Nicholas Negroponte, Brian Tracy, Simon Orebi Gann, Stephen Covey, Nelson Mandela, Gamaliel Onasode, Mahatma Gandhi, Kwame Nkrumah and others I revere. I acknowledge my family, friends, employees, partners, followers, and supporters of this book for their help in the process of writing and creating it.

I acknowledge the divine energy and higher powers that have sustained me on my life's journey and with the conception, writing and production of this book. Finally, and most importantly, I acknowledge you, my reader, for receiving the message in this book and using it in the most positive value-creating way that you know how to enhance the human race.

Notes to the Reader

About the Author

Harry 'Tomi Davies (TD) is Collaborator-in-Chief (CiC)' at TVC Labs, an entrepreneurship support organisation in Lagos, Nigeria which he founded.

TD is co-founder of the Lagos Angel Network (LAN), Chairman of the Diaspora Angels Network (DAN), founding President of the African Business Angel Network (ABAN) and board member of the Global Business Angel Network (GBAN).

After graduating from the University of Miami in 1982, TD led innovative technology-enabled transformation initiatives for influential global brands such as Elf Aquitaine, Marks & Spencer, Ernst & Young and Sapient across Europe, the United States and Southeast Asia.

In 2000, his focus shifted to Africa where he worked on various technology-led innovation initiatives in Nigeria, South Africa, Ghana, and Kenya, using his goal-oriented approach to project delivery, which inspired his 2014 book "The African Project Manager".

TD is Chairman of TextNigeria (Telecoms) and Powerstove (Renewables). He is a Non-Executive Director at MBO Capital (Private Equity), Big Cabal Media (Media & Entertainment), and Laptops4Learning (L4L) Nigeria (Edutech NGO). He also Chairs the Innovation Committee of the Lagos State Science, Research and Innovation Council (LASRIC) as well as the Innovation Support Network (ISN).

As a thought leader with insights gained from a growing portfolio of tech-enabled startup ventures originating from Africa, his personal goal is simply to "Find, Fund & Follow into the Future", African founders who are using technology-enabled innovation to create economic value and social impact across the continent. It is for them that he has written this book.

In December 2021, TD was named as one of the "100 Most Influential Africans of 2021" by New African. He can be reached at www.tomidavies.com and on LinkedIn, Twitter, Instagram and Facebook as TomiDee.

Preamble:
The POEM Framework

The African Startup Funding Challenge

African tech startups are not receiving sufficient funding and the ones that do get funding don't have as good a chance of becoming successful as their global counterparts.

Globally, all startups face the same basic set of challenges which are:

- Poor market research
- Incorrect business model
- Poor pricing strategies
- Wrong motive(s) to start the business
- Poor execution
- Unwillingness to adapt to changing market conditions

And as you have probably discovered, funding your startup idea is not an easy nut to crack. Whether

approaching incubators, accelerators, angel investors
or venture capital firms, startups globally come across
multiple hurdles when in search of funds.

African startup founders have an even bigger set of
challenges due to:

- Lack of technology infrastructure such as:
  - Power
  - Connectivity
  - R&D
  - IP Rights
- Sporadic government support programmes
- Increasing talent drain to diaspora
- Inconsistent standards across
  entrepreneurial support organisations
- Unpredictable policy and regulatory
  compliance requirements

Overcoming these funding challenges is vital if
startups are to secure the capital they need over time.
The only way startup founders can overcome these local
challenges is to leverage available ecosystem support.

There is, therefore, a need for an ecosystem that
supports these startup ventures through every step of
their development, from pre-seed funding at incubation
to seed funding for acceleration and scaling, then on to
Series A and beyond. This ecosystem needs to be built

around the unique challenges faced by our founders in Africa.

What exactly is a Startup?

According to Investopedia, "a startup is a young company founded by one or more entrepreneurs to develop a unique product or service and bring it to market. By its nature, the typical startup tends to be a shoestring operation, with initial funding from the founders or their friends and families."

According to Wikipedia, "a startup or start-up is a company or project undertaken by an entrepreneur to seek, develop and validate a scalable business model. While entrepreneurship refers to all new businesses, including self-employment and businesses that never intend to become registered, startups refer to new businesses that intend to grow large beyond the solo founder." Interswitch, MTN, MainOne, Flutterwave and Jumia were all startups at one time.

So, for the purpose of this book, our definition of a startup is: an entrepreneurial venture in its early stages of operations, built for rapid growth in extreme uncertainty, and aimed at bringing to market an innovative product or service that benefits a significant customer base economically and socially.

Startups are different from traditional, new, small business ventures in at least three critical areas – growth rate, access to funding and capital exits.

Startup Growth: In comparison to traditional business ventures, startups are expected to grow rapidly and, in Africa, at a rate of between 10% and 20% per month when in their growth-to-scale stages.

Startup Funding: Unlike SMEs, whose risk profile is known and, therefore, can obtain funding from commercial banks, startups have innovative solutions and untried business models associated with high risk. Consequently, raising funding from family, friends, fans, Angels, venture capital and private equity is the norm.

Startup Exits: Right from the beginning, startup founders must consider the exit path for their investors as a critical part of their financial strategy. All investors want to know when and how they will get their money back BEFORE they invest. SMEs have no such constraints on their planning.

The exit stage of a startup's growth is typically when the startup wants to attract additional investment for growth or wants to sell out and no longer manage the business. For investors, an "exit" occurs when the investors decide to sell their stake in a company. If an investor "exits", they will then make either a profit or a loss (obviously, they hope for a profit!).

According to Investopedia, an exit strategy is a contingency plan that is executed by an investor, venture capitalist, or business owner to liquidate a position in a financial asset or dispose of tangible business assets, once predetermined criteria for either have been met or exceeded. The most common routes to exit for startups are selling to another larger company, merging with a smaller, similar sized or larger company, or going public with an initial public offering (IPO), which occurs least often.

What's the Startup Journey?

You start with Pre-seed funding by FFF and Angels.

The earliest stage of funding for a startup comes so early in the journey that it is not generally included in rounds of funding as a "proper" round. Generally known as "pre-seed" funding, this stage typically refers to the period during which you as founders begin to get your startup operations off the ground.

At this stage of the business, your focus is on matching your startup's business opportunity with your skills, experience, and passions as the founders. Other focal points include deciding on your business ownership structure, finding professional advisors, and business planning.

The most common "pre-seed" funders of startups are the founders themselves, their family and friends (FFF), fans and angel investors. Depending on the nature of your startup and the initial costs associated with developing its minimum viable product/service

(MVP), this funding stage can happen very quickly within months or take more than a few years.

Then it's Seed Stage Funding by Angels and Early VC.

Seed is usually the first official external equity funding that a startup venture raises. The MVP would have been delivered to critical market acclaim and deemed successful. At this stage, your startup's focus should be on establishing a customer base and market presence, along with tracking and conserving cash flow.

Founders are most likely to have underestimated money needs and the time taken to access the market, so the main challenge will be not to burn through what little cash your startup venture may have raised. You will need to learn what your customers need and match that with an offer your startup can profitably deliver at a unit level. This will ensure the growth that gives potential investors confidence in funding your startup.

The most common investors for seed funding beyond founders, family, friends, fans, and hubs (incubators/accelerators) are business angel investors and early-stage venture capital companies who understand startups and expect an equity stake in your startup in exchange for their investment.

Growth Stage Funding is serious VC business.

The growth stage is the period during which the product eventually and increasingly gains acceptance as revenues and customers increase, providing new opportunities and issues. Revenue is strong, but competition is surfacing. The biggest challenge startup founders face at the growth stage is dealing with the constant range of issues bidding for their time and money. Effective management is required and, possibly, a new business strategy. As a founder, you must learn how to train talent and delegate to conquer this stage of development.

With investor involvement, founders become focused on running the business in a more formal fashion to deal with the increased sales and customers. Better accounting and management systems usually need to be set up and new employees hired to deal with the influx of business. Funding by angel syndicates, networks and funds, venture capital, grants and even banks, are all funding options for growth stage startups, depending on their rate of growth, the industry sector and, of course, the market environment.

Scale-up Funding is the Big Leagues.

Scaling your startup venture is characterised by growth from adding new products or services to your existing markets or expanding an existing business into new markets and customer types, to gain a larger market share and find new revenue and profit channels. Moving into new markets requires planning and research and, as a founder, you should focus on areas that complement your existing experience and capabilities.

Series A funding enables startups that have potential for such growth but lack cash to expand their operations through hiring, purchasing inventory and equipment, and pursuing other long-term goals required for such expansion.

Series A (B, C, D...) funding brings investments in the millions of dollars and your startup will draw this level of funding only after it has demonstrated a viable business model with strong scaling potential. Funders at this stage typically gain a large or controlling interest in the startup in exchange for their investment and the risk they are taking.

How do you measure Progress?

As African founders, innovation hubs, business angels, venture capital and other ecosystem members journey together to commercial success with founders of technology-enabled startup ventures from MVP to Series A, my POEM Framework® provides them with a simple model to meet their needs for structure, understanding, and communication with the startup venture during each stage of its lifecycle.

It provides clear metrics against which they can objectively assess the startup's progress over time, as well as helping founders understand which investors to approach when seeking capital at different stages in their lifecycle. By doing so, the framework ensures everyone associated with the startup understands what they're supposed to be doing at any given time, thereby avoiding the common risks that result in poor performance or even failure.

The five elements of the POEM Framework® are:

Vision is the founder's story about the problem or challenge and their innovation-driven commercial solution to it as a startup business venture.

Proposition is the startup's offer of products (and/or services) to the target customer base in a specific market.

Organisation is the startup's people, processes and technologies that deliver the proposition.

Economics measure the startup's use of available capital for funding expenses to generate revenues that create impact.

Milestones measure the startup's targets, challenges, and achievements from MVP to Series A.

To start and sustain a successful startup in Africa, as in any other place, the startup founder requires a compelling vision that will drive the execution of all the activities required to bring that vision to life as a successful business venture.

The life of that startup is measured by its achievements as it overcomes challenges to progress towards the realisation of that vision. It is this journey to the successful delivery of the vision by the founders that early-stage investors seek to join and help along the way in exchange for returns from the expected outcomes.

Because founders, hubs and investors alike are primarily interested in exploiting the commercial and social potential of the venture, by necessity, the focus is on how:

The product/service offer makes money by solving a significant problem or meeting a critical need for a specific set of customers in a target market,

Delivery of the technology-enabled product/ service offer to satisfy those customers is profitably achieved with social impact.

This book provides details of the POEM Framework® for those founders with a vision of their own, whether just beginning, or already on that journey from minimum viable product and your first customer, through the first funding round to Series A and beyond... I trust it helps!

TD - September 2022

CHAPTER 1

Tell your story!

Traits of the successful founder

Every startup begins with the founders, those amazing individuals like you, inspired enough to dedicate time, effort and money towards bringing their vision of a startup venture to life.

They have driven investment in African startups from $100 million in 2015 to over $5 billion in 2021. This rare breed of people we call entrepreneurs are as diverse as there are ventures on the continent, with success stories having similarities yet uniqueness.

Founders need to have certain personality traits for their startups to become successful. To put it very simply, if you want to start a business, which is what a startup is, then you need to be the kind of person who can run one. Some traits that successful startup founders have in common include:

Persistence – Startup founders know how to put a lot of energy into their work despite the setbacks and challenges they may face along the way. Successful startup founders can focus on their goals without being distracted by things around them that they cannot influence.

Optimism – Startup founders are generally very optimistic about the future of their business idea, even when multiple challenges arise. They are also able to see opportunities where others may only see problems. This applies not only to situations related specifically to your startup's product or service but also to various social and economic factors that could affect its success as a business.

Passion – Startup founders are generally passionate about their product or service and believe in its potential. This passion is what convinces them to put so much energy into developing a successful startup; they have complete confidence that it will succeed. Founders having this trait can convince others, both inside and outside of their startup team, also to hold this conviction in their product or service.

Drive – Being passionate about your startup idea isn't enough for you to be able to achieve success with the idea. As a startup founder, you need a certain level of drive, or motivation, to take action when lacking information or when you're faced with challenges. You must be driven to achieve your vision, whatever it takes.

Intelligence – As a startup founder, you will need to make decisions based on information available to you, whether or not that information is complete. Successful founders can plan the best course of action despite lacking some important data points. This trait also applies to emotional intelligence; being aware of your own emotions and how they affect decision-making. Being intelligent also means being resourceful, finding creative solutions to problems.

Openness – This trait is all about being open to new experiences, activities and situations that are important for developing as an entrepreneur and personally. Successful startup founders often explore beyond their comfort zone when necessary. They can be flexible and adapt quickly.

Focus – Startup founders need the ability to focus on what is important, instead of being distracted by things that don't matter as much or aren't as relevant. You must be able to keep your team focused on goals despite outside challenges or obstacles they will no doubt face along the way.

Integrity – Startup founders need to be able to make sound decisions and communicate them effectively. You also need to communicate honestly with your employees, partners and customers. This trait is closely related to open-mindedness, and differences of opinion shouldn't distract startup founders from staying focused on what matters most and communicating those issues.

These personality traits that are needed to be a successful founder are not necessarily something you are born with. It is possible to develop them over time through certain experiences and exposure to personalities, enabling you to survive the startup journey from early struggle to long-term success.

Know what makes you an ideal African founder

To understand what makes a successful African founder, let's look at the key traits I've personally observed in some of our inspiring Nigerian startup founders. I have had the privilege of knowing people like Funke Opeke (Main One), Iyin Aboyeji (Andela, Flutterwave & Future.Africa), Tayo Oviosu (Paga), Bosun Tijani (ccHub), and Sim Shagaya (DealDay, Konga & uLesson), who are each in their own uniquely individual way:

Visionaries, capable of bringing their vision to life through a realistic perspective on the work and time required to build their startup company.

Passionate leaders, who are knowledgeable about running an organisation, know what's needed, are aware they don't have all the skills required but have access to the requisite resources for execution.

Managers, who can clearly explain the delivery of organisational structure, including the roles and responsibilities of the board, management, key staff and partners.

Executives, who understand the importance of attracting an effective board of directors and advisers to fill in gaps in expertise and experience in the venture's leadership.

Self-aware individuals who have challenging yet realistic goals.

Being the successful founder of a startup venture means having the right attitude towards delivering your business vision and the determination, grit and openness to learning and the change required to achieve success.

These founders have a strong inner drive that helps them flourish. Excited by the prospect of rewarding work, they have a strong ambition to succeed and overcome obstacles. They not only set aspiring goals for themselves but are totally committed to achieving them, regardless of the countless challenges they encounter.

Each one of them has a strong sense of self-confidence and a healthy opinion not only of their skills and abilities but also of their shortcomings. Their assertive and strong personalities mean they are always focused and do not really dilly-dally with the issues at hand. This is what makes them different from the rest.

These great founders are always on the lookout for new innovations and ideas that are potential winners. They constantly reinvent themselves with a focus on better ways to run their businesses and improve the products and services they offer.

A critically important quality of great founders is their openness to adopting positive change. They tend not to be headstrong or stubborn when it comes to choosing alternative options. Approaching challenges with an open mind and eagerness to learn new things, they understand that to stay ahead of the pack, they must keep evolving with the times by exploiting the latest methods and technologies to serve their customers better.

Competition is what great founders thrive on for improvisation and change, with some even using competitors' activities for motivation. This ability and being able to accept both rejection and constructive criticism equally, go a long way in making these founders successful.

The bottom line is great founders are emotionally intelligent, self-aware, and high achievers! My question is: Are you?

Know yourself well enough to tell them about you

"Who are you and what's your story?" is the most common question founders are asked when they present their startup to investors for the first time. This may be one of the most important questions about what your startup venture will become, as knowing yourself helps create a more successful startup by attracting people who are right for your journey.

When this question is asked, you must be prepared to share enough about yourself and your background to help the investor get to know you well enough to build a sense of why you are particularly suited to building your startup.

Let's get started, with you taking some time out to answer these questions about yourself in writing:

Who are you?

A founder's ideas, motivation, attitude and performance result from their core value drivers which, when in alignment with the right support (at the right time) from the right investors, can actually determine their startup's chances of success. Focus on what makes up your core values and how they drive your entrepreneurial behaviour.

Once you have and can demonstrate a good understanding of who you are at the core (essential you), it becomes easier to attract the kind of people who will enable your startup's journey to success.

...and what's your story?

Your geographical origins, early years, educational, vocational, professional and other life experiences are what makes you a unique individual, so it's important you catalogue, categorise and document them in ways that are relevant and easy to share with others.

Be sure to include relevant personalities and events that have helped bring you to where you are today. Don't shy away from the challenges you've had to overcome too, especially those that were pertinent to your startup's genesis, remembering this is about you as an entrepreneur, not just your startup idea or business!

As a founder in today's world, your LinkedIn and social media profiles (e.g. Twitter, Facebook, Instagram, etc.) are the first places potential investors look to understand your background and life experiences. Make sure these digital fingerprints tell your story well.

Sharing your journey so far, with the business and personal achievements you've enjoyed and how they came about, is something you should get used to doing as a founder.

The rendering of yourself and the relevant experiences you've had on your life journey is extremely important when you first meet potential investors as well as co-founders, employees and partners, so review and reflect on it regularly, remembering you never get a second chance to make a good first impression.

CHAPTER 2

Share the future you see!

The question of what exactly it is you're building, assessing, and learning should start with some old-fashioned thinking about what you see in the future—YOUR VISION! It means walking yourself through a process that recognises you're preparing to build or may already be building a business (again that's exactly what your startup is!) that could change the world!

To help others assess the viability of your vision, you should be able to articulate it as a tangible problem or challenge for a set of human beings, with your personal story providing the solution as a startup business. So, once more, what's the problem or challenge you see and what, exactly, is your innovative solution to it?

Every successful founder has a vision of the potential inherent in their startup's future and how they imagine it will pan out. Your primary job as a founder in this case is to share your vision in a way that shows others that solving the problem or meeting the challenge you have identified creates economic value and social impact in the market you have chosen to serve.

To have a clear vision for your startup, you need to be certain about the problem or challenge being addressed and the opportunity it creates for your startup solution. This should include an understanding of the people it could or would affect and in what way. You should become intimately familiar with how those affected by this problem or challenge manage it currently. This will help you to develop insights into the competitive landscape.

If you have not done so already, let me help you get started by asking you to think through and write down your answers to these starter questions:

Have a clear vision for your startup

Founder - that's you!

- What exactly is the problem I am solving and why does it exist?

- Why do I want to start (or continue) this startup business?

- What are my goals (personal and business)?

- Am I ready to invest the time needed in this startup?

- Am I motivated and passionate enough about this to work on it for a decade?

My Startup's Proposition:

- For whom does my solution create value?
- Why is it valuable to them?
- How many of them are there?
- What is my Unique Selling Proposition (USP)?
- Who are my competitors?

My Startup's Organisation:

- Who else will help me build this startup?
- What kind of legal structure should my startup adopt?
- How many employees will we need?
- How will we market our startup?
- How will we find and serve our customers?
- What kind of tech will we need to deploy?

My Startup's Economics:

- What resources do I already have available?
- What funds do I need to start and run this startup business?

- How profitable can this startup be now and in the future?

- What's it going to cost to generate the revenues I envisage?

- What kind of taxes will I have to pay?

- What impact will my startup have on the lives of our customers and others (economic and social)?

My Startup's Milestones:

- When will I start building the startup?

- When will I expect to find my first customer?

- When will I look forward to meeting my first investor?

- How will we look in 10 years' time?

The answers to these questions, when reviewed, will tell you if you really have a workable vision for your startup and how best to articulate it.

The final result of this thought process should be a vision statement that you can share with everyone who comes into contact with your startup, from your co-founders (who may help construct the statement) to employees, customers, partners and investors.

To be sure you've established a credibly viable vision for your startup, let's take a closer look in more detail at the problem/challenge, the people it would affect and how they would cope.

Know how big the problem or challenge is

The problem or challenge you are addressing is at the heart of your startup idea, so that's where you start. It's what intrigues people about your business and ultimately becomes the focal point for everything you build.

So, before you begin your startup, ask yourself: "What problem or challenge are we addressing?" Why is this question so important? It's important because you can never build anything bigger than the problem or challenge you're trying to address with your venture.

The problem or challenge could be financial, health and well-being, environmental, logistical, educational, economic, or social, so the next critical question is: "Are we solving a meaningful problem on both the demand and supply sides, or at least on one of them?" (Or are you simply attempting to foist another copycat competitor onto an already overcrowded marketplace?)

After you've answered these starter questions, you'll need to follow up by answering other relevant questions, including but not limited to:

- Is the problem local, national, regional, continental, or global?
- Why does this problem exist?

- What opportunities does the problem/challenge present?

- Who would be the beneficiaries of a possible solution?

- Would they have the capability and authority to pay for a solution?

- What other similar problems/challenges do they have today?

The answers to these questions, when reviewed, will give you clarity as to the problem/challenge your startup will address and how best to articulate it. The final result of this thought process should be a clear understanding of the problem or challenge articulated in a statement that you can share with interested parties to support your vision statement. Before you start focusing on market size, you should calculate and review the size of your problem, which you obtain by multiplying frequency, intensity, and the potential number of users (Problem Size = Frequency x Intensity x Users).

Frequency: how often do users experience this problem? Daily, weekly, monthly, annually, biennially, every decade?

Intensity: how much are customers already paying in terms of time or money for alternative solutions?

Users: potentially how many people or businesses have this problem?

Your problem statement should then include the size of the problem. For example:

People need to get from point A to B within a 10-mile radius to go to work, school, church, mosque, events, restaurants, airport and more:

Frequency: two-four times per day

Intensity: consumers buy cars to solve this problem and the average cost of car ownership is $500/month

The extent of users: there are 47 million people of 'working age' in Nigeria who commute daily

In considering the problem in this example, you can see you would be trying to solve a huge problem as millions of Nigerians spend over $6,000 ($500 x 12 months) per year on running a car.

Problem Size = 4 x 500 x 47,000,000 = $94B

It is necessary to carry out sampling to ascertain the size of the problem as you should always use data (primary or secondary) arising from your own research carried out to the required level to validate any assumptions.

With questions answered, research done and the problem statement in tow, you are ready to assist the people affected by the problem.

Understand the people that the problem affects

To create a successful startup, it's important to first understand the problem you're trying to solve. This problem statement will determine who is affected by your solution, and why you need to thoroughly understand what the needs of the people affected are.

For example, if you're creating a new messaging app, your problem statement might be something like, "How can we make it easier for people to stay in touch with their friends and family?" This problem statement would affect anyone who wants to stay in touch with friends and family, regardless of where they are located.

It's also important to understand how the problem or challenge affects the people concerned. For example, if your problem statement is "How can we make it easier for people to stay in touch with their friends and family?" you might think that the biggest challenge is getting people to download your app. However, if your target audience is busy working professionals who are already overloaded with notifications, you need to design your app to minimise distractions and make it easy to send a message quickly.

Understanding your problem statement is essential to creating a successful startup. By knowing whom you're trying to help and how the problem affects them, you can focus on solving the right problem and making a difference in people's lives. It's not enough to know that there is a problem out there. You need to drill down and understand the specific needs of the people affected by it. Only then can you start to develop a solution that meets those needs.

Your problem statement is the foundation of your startup. It determines whom you are targeting and how you are going to solve their problem. You must get it right, and that starts with understanding the people who need your help. So don't just go out and ask people what problem they want to be solved. Talk to them about the problem they are currently struggling with. Ask them how they manage it and why it's a problem for them. Only then will you be able to develop a solution that is wanted and needed.

If you can get this right, you'll be well on your way to building a successful startup. It is important that you fully understand those affected as they have the potential to become your startup's customers. What do they do for a living? Where do they hang out? Where would you expect to find them, and in which kinds of shops, stores, and public places? How and why do they currently manage the problem?

You can then group these potential customers according to their demographics, such as age, race, gender, education, income level and geographical location. Psychographic information (including values and personality traits) and behavioural information should help you develop the profiles of your potential customer base.

Behavioural segmentation can also help you understand how people will adapt to your startup's solution. You should try to understand what motivates them to look for a new solution to the problem and why they may not be using their current solution to full effect.

To validate your profiles, sampling research (both desk and field) should be carried out to document the findings of the people affected by the problem. The research should give you an insight into how these people solve their problems currently, uncovering information that will help you target your solution more effectively. It should also help you create and deepen customer relationships and reach untapped customer populations to increase the reach of your startup.

Identify current solutions to the problem/challenge

The use of market, user and competitor research is crucial in learning how the problem can be dealt with today and who your competitors are, in order to gain a clear understanding of the current solutions. You must learn which products and services in the target market and customer base are similar to your solution because they will be your competition.

Looking at your market, many entrepreneurs undertake only a minimal amount of market research. It is vital to conduct both primary and secondary market research into your startup business concept to fully understand its feasibility as a project based on the target market information.

By conducting primary research on appropriately selected individuals and groups from your existing and potential customer base, you can gain the latest insights into their wants and needs, allowing you to adapt your product or service offering accordingly to gain a competitive advantage.

Secondary market research will give you an overview of your market and the historical success of similar products and services in addition to your target market's previous purchasing habits.

Conducting market research has many benefits for startup founders. The key advantages are unbiased views, reliable data, valid results and actual figures. Startups, for example, are presented with a series of barriers to overcome when seeking credit. Primary research can help remove some of these. Unbiased information obtained from the primary market research you conduct yourself will enable you to build a product or service offering, which will meet your customers' needs in ways others cannot.

Some questions to ask yourself and how to resolve them:

- How much do you know?
- How do people solve the problem today?
- What other solutions are available to them?
- What is the cost/benefit analysis resulting from the current solution?

- How much information is missing?
- Gather information on the problem.
- Compare the current solutions to yours.
- How may the solutions for the two problems be different?

Articulate your startup's solution

So now we know the problem, we want a new solution that will solve the problem but, most importantly, one that's going to be profitable and have an impact. This means clearly defining the solution you are offering.

Be sure it's an innovative solution

While we tend to think of innovation as new technology, innovative solutions can also come in the form of new types of services that offer improvements on traditional methods, meet previously unidentified needs or fill gaps in the market.

The best solutions tend to be a combination of technological services, tools, and techniques. Startups typically focus their innovative solutions on a given niche depending on the problem that the founders are aiming to solve in the market.

Unique Selling Proposition (USP) - Focus on the questions around the solution because the USP concerns what, how, and why you are selling your product or service. The answers should match the unique selling proposition points.

Your USP is what sets you apart from your competitors!

Identify your USP in 7 simple steps:

- Step 1: Brainstorm ideas.

- Step 2: Identify your customers.

- Step 3: Analyse your competitors.

- Step 4: List your strengths.

- Step 5: Know your weaknesses.

- Step 6: Figure out what makes you unique.

- Step 7: Frame your USP in the most appropriate words.

In formulating your USP, it helps to ask yourself the following questions:

- What benefits will our customers receive?

- Can we sell to this market, or type of buyer, and maintain profitability?

- To summarise—there are four elements to your USP:

  - Know your audience, buyer profile and ideal customer. Be aware of what motivates them and why.

o   Solve a genuine problem. There are many problems still to be solved – the market is changing, almost on an exponential scale compared to 100 years ago.

o   Demonstrate unique benefits. Make sure you deliver on these benefits.

o   Acquire paying customers as soon as possible. Ok, this isn't quite part of your USP, but it helps to have some early adopters on whom you can test your USP. If needed, you can iterate your offer to suit the market and drive further growth.

An innovative solution to the problem!

You need to make sure you validate your solution to ensure it solves the problem.

To solve a problem, there are basic steps to take which include identifying the problem, generating new ideas, evaluating, and selecting the solutions and, lastly, validating and implementing the final result/outcome to determine if it solves the problem you have identified.

Just as there are mechanisms for solving problems, there exist different methods to determine whether your solution solves the problem:

•   Define the problem

•   Analyse the problem

•   Describe the solution

- Develop alternative solutions
- Implement the chosen solution
- Measure the results

An innovative solution that makes money!

Everyone wants to know if a great idea will be profitable. The first factor you have to consider is the customer, with whom you form revenue-generating segment relationships using channel communications. A business model describes the value an organisation offers its customers. It illustrates the capabilities and resources required to create, market, and deliver this value, and to generate profitable, sustainable revenue streams.

The business model is the key factor that leads to success in startups. It provides the starting point that enables a company to maximise its profit. The sooner the business model is in place, the better. Using the business model canvas will lead to insights into the customers you serve, what value propositions are offered through which channels, and how your company becomes profitable.

The business model canvas is divided into four segments: Customer, Product, Profitability and People.

- **Customer:** Forming revenue-generating segment relationships using channel communications

- **Product:** Development and delivery of value-creating units to customers

- **Profitability:** Freemium to premium fees for revenue-generating activities and resource expenses

- **People:** Expertise required (including partners) for running daily business operations.

The model focuses on coordinating internal and external processes to determine how the startup interacts with stakeholder partners, distribution channels and customers.

At its core, your business model is how your business makes money. It's...

- How you deliver value to your customers at an appropriate cost

- What it takes to make your solution in terms of product design and development, and human resources

- What it takes to sell the solution to customers with regard to marketing, distribution, service delivery, sales processing, and customer support

- How and what customers pay for the solution in respect of pricing strategy, payment methods and timing

the list continues...

An innovative solution that creates impact!

Potential impact is becoming increasingly important. There are 17 Sustainable Development Goals contained in three layers. Each of the SDGs falls within the three layers. Although the SDGs differ from each other, they are also interconnected and support each other. To achieve sustainability, all three layers (Biosphere/ Environment, Society, and Economy) must be actioned by a startup.

Layer One is the biosphere that encompasses the whole world. For example, climate change is something many people believe affects the global environment. This layer is the foundation, and if not healthy and free from harm, cannot benefit society and the global economy.

Layer Two is society and the aims that would improve people's lives include zero hunger and good health and well-being, all of which are societal developmental goals. Society exists within and is supported by the environment.

Layer Three is the economy that includes work, employment, and economic growth, which depend on industrial and technological innovation and adequate infrastructure and are the by-products that are supported by society. These are the three layers of impact, which you need to understand in the context of how your startup corresponds to these SDG goals and the effect they could have.

Employment and economic growth are factors that will be relevant to your startup.

Here are the 17 SDGs:

- No Poverty
- Zero Hunger
- Good health and well-being
- Quality education
- Gender equality
- Clean water and sanitation
- Affordable and clean energy
- Purposeful work and economic growth
- Industry, innovation, and infrastructure
- Reduced inequalities
- Sustainable cities and communities
- Responsible use of resources and methods of production
- Climate action
- Life below water
- Life on land
- Peace, justice, and robust institutions
- Partnerships for achieving the goals

Sustainability focuses on meeting human needs within ecological constraints. Economic decisions can form part of a strategy to increase profitability while achieving greater sustainability.

Know how to bring your solution to life

Now that we have a solution, let's look at thinking it through to bring it to life. Design thinking is the method of creating human-focused solutions through convergent and divergent thinking.

Innovation = Convergence + Divergence

Convergence: A left-brain thinker is systematic and meticulous. The left hemisphere of the brain is responsible for computing data and linear thinking. When tackling problems, a left-brain thinker reviews evidence-based research to find a logical solution. This style of problem-solving, called convergent thinking, is the process of analysing a mass of information to arrive at one definite solution.

Divergence: Responsible for creative thinking, the right hemisphere of the brain approaches problems with a sense of curiosity. While searching for a solution, a right-brain thinker will turn a problem into a question and start brainstorming. This process, called divergent thinking, is driven by a desire to pursue several possibilities through the spontaneous generation of ideas.

Design thinking is being adopted by contemporary organisations, which use these strategies to help solve problems and become, in effect, global design and innovation companies.

Five steps for creating innovative ideas | The design-thinking approach

Step One: Empathise

Understanding your user's needs to gather insights means actively listening and setting aside previous assumptions, or unconscious bias. Think outside the box and look for information beyond the user. Often, related environments and relationships will provide helpful facts for you to consider. Understanding the purpose and choosing the right tool for your data collection is important in achieving the desired results. Surveys, conversations, and observations are a few worthwhile options. This step uses divergent thinking and is key to constructing the basis of your solution.

Step Two: Define

Apply convergent thinking to the data and frame the problem with humanistic language. Clearly identify what you're addressing and avoid being too broad or too specific in the problem statement. Take the time to concentrate on the real issue and be careful of getting distracted by easy-to-fix symptoms.

Step Three: Imagine

Let your creative juices flow! After defining the problem, it's time to start brainstorming. Have fun at this stage. Don't leave any possible or impossible solutions off the table. For example, if you think ice farming in the Sahara Desert will fix the problem, write it down. As ideas accumulate, they will spark further ideas and possibly lead you to a solution you would never have considered. Needless to say, divergent thinking is used at this stage and moves you closer to an innovative solution.

Step Four: Build a prototype

After reviewing your creative ideas, select one or two solutions you want to pursue. After deciding to move ahead, it's time to create a small-scale prototype, typically an inexpensive model of what a real product or service would be. Examples could be a mock-up of a new website, an outline for a novel, or a beta version of a piece of software. Move on to the next stage in the knowledge that your prototype isn't perfect and will likely need modifications.

Step Five: Test

Testing allows you to modify your prototype before sending it to production. Even if it needs modifications, or fails completely, the flexibility granted by design thinking lets you return to previous stages without wasting too many precious resources. Organisations using this process are fully aware they are able to create an innovative solution more quickly and cheaply through iteration than by using the conventional convergent problem-solving approaches.

Questions to ask yourself so you can respond to investors and interested parties, when asked about building your startup's solution, include:

- How would you describe your solution in one sentence?

- How innovative is your solution?

- How does it create value for the intended users?

- What makes it exclusive and hard for others to match?

- How do you know the intended users will value your solution?

What's unique about your solution? A specific position that forces you to make a case against competing products is more memorable than a generic stance, such as: "We sell high-quality products."

- What do your customers value? Which innovation in your solution do your target customers really care about?

- What makes your solution different? Who are your competitors and what exactly are you doing differently (and/or better) than them?

- How will your solution make money?
- What are the risks and challenges you expect to overcome?

So now that you've established you have a vision for your startup, the next step is to answer the question: "How do you intend to bring your vision to life?" How do you as a visionary founder articulate your entrepreneurial journey to commercial success?

The answer is to write a POEM profile for your vision based on the results of the thought process and research (desk and field) you have carried out and discussions you should have had about your startup, and the industry or industry segment(s) in which it will actualise your vision. Now let's dive in to see what its details look like.

PROPOSITION

In the previous chapter, I helped establish that you do have a vision for your startup. The next step in building your startup is to answer the question: "How do you intend to bring your vision to life"? How do you as a visionary articulate the entrepreneurial journey to commercial success?

The answer is to write a POEM profile for your vision based on the results of the thinking and research (desk and field) you have done and discussions you should have had about your startup and the industry or industry segment(s) in which it will actualise your vision. Your POEM profile should comprehensively describe your business vision and can be used to do so throughout your startup's life cycle from ideation to institutional investment. The Proposition, Organisation, Economics and Milestones: each add a piece to the story of your startup and together describe it totally.

We'll start with the P, for the Proposition your startup is making to the world it will operate in. The instinctive approach is to elaborate on the product or service offering, but I recommend you start with a thorough understanding of the context for your business proposition. Specifically, I recommend that you familiarise yourself with the market and where appropriate, the industry segment you intend to operate in. Be sure you get to know what's happening in it today (i.e. key trends and issues) and what the outlook for it is, including any new products and developments. You must be able to articulate what the prospects are and how all of these will benefit or adversely affect your startup business as it brings your vision to life.

Your understanding of the market context will stand you in good stead for the next step in the process, which is the conceptual development in as much detail as you can at this very early stage of your product or service offering. Think through and develop your ideas about its features, functions, and the kind of customer experience you intend it to deliver. Most importantly, be sure you know and can describe the value proposition it will deliver to your customers.

Now that you have a product or service value proposition and an understanding of the industry in which it will be delivered, you should forensically analyse the different aspects of the market segment that your startup will be targeting. I recommend an in-depth analysis of the different customer profiles you intend to attract and retain for your revenues. At the very least, this should include some basic demographic and psychographic analysis of each group.

Next up on your Proposition checklist of fact gathering and data analysis is the competitor landscape for your startup. Big or small, old or new, be sure to identify the types of competitors with actual examples of each type and their operations. Analyse the strengths and weaknesses of each identified competitor or type and think through how your startup intends to differentiate itself against them to build your business, remembering that documentation of the facts, analysis and conclusions are key.

Be sure you identify any regulatory compliance requirements that will affect your startup, as well as any dependencies you will have on others for input into your product or service development and delivery. The earlier in the process you can identify and bed down any issues associated with suppliers, contractors, and compliance, the easier your life will be further down the line.

Finally, you should think through and devise the strategies that you believe will give you a clear advantage in the industry, build barriers for new entrants, and exploit the weaknesses you identified in the incumbents.

When you have gone through this process and can honestly say you have executed each step with passion using all that is at your disposal, the result should be a well-articulated Proposition to a clearly defined customer base in a known market that will generate sustainable revenue with impact while bringing your startup vision to life.

CHAPTER 3

Become familiar with your market.

Know your startup's market!

Really getting to know your startup's market is a critical step in the process of initiating your startup because it allows you to determine whether or not there's enough room for growth within any already-established industry.

Not only does this give you insight into the size of your potential market but it also helps you as a founder know if there are viable competitors with existing companies that provide similar services to yours!

"Market opportunity" is defined as a need or demand in a market that a company can capitalise on by introducing a new product or service.

Market Size looks at the size of your specific target market, which means finding the relevant statistics about your industry segment, which takes time and effort, but finding the right statistics for the key metrics makes all the difference to investors.

Key metrics are those that are specifically relevant to your market and can be anything specifically related to your industry sector. You should determine which metrics and statistics investors would be most interested in knowing about your industry, keeping in mind that information needs to be relevant.

Of critical importance will be the market's growth rate which will determine your startup's potential and can be determined by comparing it to growth rates in similar markets to provide perspective.

A key part of operating any business is understanding the industry and the market it is serving. That means analysing the competition, the opportunity for growth and your customer base.

You need to understand how business is done in your industry, the ways in which products are sold and delivered, and what terms and conditions are offered by other players (i.e. your competitors).

The location, landscape, people, culture, and activities of the land shape and define the geography of a market.

Location & Landscape

Which villages, towns, cities, countries, regions, and continents will we operate in? The physical location and visible features of the land and how they integrate with natural or man-made resources.

People & Culture

Who are the people in those locations?

The human population distribution, their grouping characteristics and knowledge, including language, religion, cuisine, social habits, music and arts.

Political & Economic Activities

What are their main market activities?

The particular political public governance and economic private sector commercial activities of the people.

Determine your market size

Market size is the number of potential customers who could buy from your business. TAM, SAM, and SOM are acronyms for three metrics to describe the market in which your startup operates.

These metrics are key components of your strategic plans, particularly as you craft your marketing and sales strategy, set realistic revenue goals, and choose to enter the markets that are worth your time and resources.

TAM (Total Attainable / Addressable Market)

How big is the largest possible market?

TAM is the total possible demand for your product or service offer without any limitations to geography, product, etc.

Total attainable market or TAM refers to the total market demand for a product or service. It's the maximum amount of revenue a business can possibly generate by selling its product or service in a specific market.

TAM is most useful for businesses to estimate objectively a specific market's potential for growth.

The best way to calculate your TAM is by running a bottom-up analysis of an industry. A bottom-up analysis involves counting the total number of customers in a market and multiplying that number by the average annual revenue of each customer in this market.

For example, let's say a startup named AutoDriver created a self-driving smartphone app, which brings in an average revenue of $500 per customer. The TAM could be all people of driving age. Assuming a world population of 7.8 billion and 72% of them are of driving age, the TAM calculation could be done as:

- TAM = 7.8 billion x 72% x $500 = $2,808 billion

SAM (Serviceable Available / Served Addressable Market)

- What portion of the market can we actually serve?

SAM is the portion of the market you can actually reach, given the limitations of product, geography, demographics, and psychographics.

SAM is most useful for businesses to estimate objectively the portion of the market they can acquire to determine their targets.

To calculate your SAM, count all the potential customers who would be a good fit for your business and multiply that number by the average annual revenue of these types of customers in your market.

If our fictional startup, AutoDriver, began operations in Nigeria and their app worked solely on Android phones, their SAM would have to take into account the car-driving population of Nigeria that has access to Android phones and can afford the app. If that population happened to be 15 million potential customers, the SAM calculation would be:

- SAM = 15 million x $500 = $7.5 billion

SOM (Serviceable Obtainable Market)

- What portion of the market do we expect to serve?

SOM is the target market share you can expect to acquire, given your go-to-market investment and competition.

SOM is most useful for businesses to determine short-term growth targets.

Sometimes SOM is also referred to as Share of Market.

As Investopedia puts it, "Market share is the percentage of total sales in an industry generated by a particular company. Market share is calculated by taking the company's sales over the period and dividing it by the total sales of the industry over the same period. This metric is used to give a general idea of the size of a company in relation to its market and its competitors. The market leader in an industry is the company with the largest market share."

To calculate your SOM, divide your revenue for the year by your industry's serviceable addressable market for the year. This percentage is your market share from last year. Then, multiply your market share from last year by your industry's serviceable addressable market from this year.

Let's assume AutoDriver was able to generate $10 million of revenue and their SAM grew to $8.5 billion, the SOM calculation would come out to:

- SOM = $10 million/$7.5 billion x $8.5 billion = $11.3 million.

Know your competition & regulations.

Understanding your startup's target market is critical to success. This means knowing the competition and regulations that currently prevail in the market your startup already operates in or plans to. Knowing the prevailing regulatory and competitive environment is crucial. Without this knowledge, you run the risk of wasting valuable time and money trying to compete in a space where your startup cannot win.

There will always be rivalry between companies selling similar products and services to the same customers, so knowing and understanding your competition is a critical step in designing a successful marketing strategy. Identifying your competition and staying informed about their products and services is the key to remaining competitive in the market and is crucial to the survival of any business.

There are two major types of Market competitors:

Direct Competitors - Who are you competing against directly?

These are the companies in the market selling the same products or services, in the same way, and at a similar price point to the same customers as your startup.

A direct competitor offers the same products and services aimed at the same target market and customer base, with the same goal of profit and market share growth. This means that your direct competitors are targeting the same audience as you, selling the same products as you, in a similar distribution model as you.

Indirect Competitors - Who are we competing against indirectly?

These are companies in the market selling alternative products or services in a different way at comparable price points to the same customers.

An indirect competitor offers the same products and services, much like direct competitors; however, the end goals are different. These competitors are seeking to grow revenue with a different strategy.

To get a clear understanding of your regulatory environment, you need to find answers to these questions:

Regulation:

Which laws and rules are our operations subject to?

Regulations include laws, rules, and standards regarding how applicable goods and services can be offered and delivered in the market and, in some cases, the level of control any given participant is allowed to assume over a market.

Compliance:

What must we do or not do to stay legal?

Compliance is the process through which you demonstrate that you have conformed to the specific requirements in laws, regulations, contracts, strategies, and policies that apply to your startup.

Standards:

Which standards are applicable to our operations?"

The prevailing standards for products, workplaces, safety, and mitigation of environmental and social impacts are considerations for the operational activities of the startup.

Identify relevant economic factors & trends.

Economic factors have a significant impact on how your startup does business and also how profitable it can be. Factors to consider about your market include - economic growth, interest rates, exchange rates, inflation and disposable income of your customers (both consumers and businesses) which can impact their spending habits.

Market trends show an alteration in these economic factors in the market where your startup operates and there are different types of trends:

Demographic:

How are people in the market changing?

What are the measurable changes perceived in the characteristics of the market's human population e.g., increased or decreased concentration of a particular ethnic group, sex ratio, etc...

Technological:

How is technology changing our market?

Which technologies have recently become popular and are being readily accepted in the market, and how useful is such technology for the success of our startup...

Economic:

What changes are there in our market's activities?

What are the recorded patterns of changes in the nature of financial transactions between the government, companies, and consumers in the market?

Questions you can expect from investors

- Where's the physical market for your startup located?

- What's the size and make of the market opportunity?

- Which industry regulations and competition currently prevail?

- What are the dominant economic factors and emerging trends?

CHAPTER 4

Understand your customers.

Successful founders really understand their customers. Knowing your target customer is half the battle when it comes to developing a successful startup. And when you understand the specific characteristics and needs of your customer base, you can deliver your solution at the right price, in the right place and in their language.

So, learning more about your customers than they know about you will put you ahead of the game in no time. First, though, you need to decide the type of customers you want for your startup which, of course, will depend to a great degree on the type of business you are running and the industry in which it operates.

For example, a startup selling complex fintech products with a relatively high price point obviously needs to appeal to customers with above-average incomes. A mass-market e-commerce startup, on the other hand, appeals to a different set of customers.

Know your customers well

To determine the type of customer you want for your startup, further analyse the market and industry you're operating in and the characteristics of the typical customers for products such as those your startup sells.

Then to know these customers better, you should use both customer profiling and segmentation, which are two sides of the same coin, albeit with subtle differences.

While customer profiling is about knowing your customers intimately enough to describe their different types (known as personas), customer segmentation is about dividing your customer base into different groups that share specific characteristics you engage with them on.

Customer profiling clusters your customers into groups based on common traits, shared goals, and similar characteristics. You then give each of the resulting customer groups an indicative name, image, and description. These are the 'personas' of who your startup's offer is for. Customer profiles are used to help your startup make customer-centred decisions without confusing expectations of the product with personal opinions.

The personas can then be used as a tool by your team to make key design decisions, e.g. "Which of these features will help Lola achieve her goals most easily?" We all know the importance of omnichannel experience—a consistent look and feel at all customer touchpoints, including bricks-and-mortar, face-to-face, online, voice phone, and mobile.

Personas, a design tool for omnichannel technology touchpoints such as websites, mobile apps, kiosks, etc. deliver that experience but are not a replacement for customer segmentation, which is used for marketing and sales. Successful customer profiling results in enhanced customer experiences, optimised retention and loyalty, and a potentially more effective marketing strategy.

Customer segmentation (CS), on the other hand, is the practice of dividing customers into groups that reflect their similarities. Using customer segments, you should be able to decide how best to relate, value-wise and otherwise, based on these groupings, to maximise profits from everyone's perspective while also ensuring good service quality for everyone involved!

The power of customer segmentation lies in the ability to tailor bitesize offers in each market individually, giving you an edge over your competition. As the possibilities for improving your startup's performance through customer segmentation are endless, you will be able to target and engage with your customers better by determining a clear set of messages and imagery for each specific customer segment.

And aside from focusing your marketing message and enabling your sales team to pursue higher quality opportunities, CS can improve your startup's product, potentially increasing revenues.

There are four different types of market segmentation.

- Where customers come from - Geographic Segmentation

- Who customers are - Demographic Segmentation

- Why customers buy - Psychographic Segmentation

- How customers buy - Behavioural Segmentation

Now let's look at each one in a little more detail.

Know where they're from (Geography)

By comparison, geographic segmentation, often one of the easiest to identify, groups customers with regard to their physical location. This can be defined in any number of ways:

- Country

- Region

- City

- Town

- Village

- Hamlet

- Postal Code

For example, customers can be grouped within a set radius of a certain location – an excellent option for marketers of live events looking to reach local audiences. Being aware of your customers' location allows for all sorts of considerations when advertising to them.

Know who they are (Demographics)

Demographic segmentation might be the first thing people think of when they hear 'market segmentation' and it is, perhaps, the most straightforward way of defining customer groups, but it remains powerful. Demographic segmentation looks at identifiable non-character traits such as:

- Age

- Gender

- Ethnicity

- Income

- Level of education

- Religion

- Profession/role in a company

For example, demographic segmentation might target potential customers based on their income, so your marketing budget isn't wasted directing your messaging at people who likely can't afford your startup's product.

Know why they buy (Psychographics)

Psychographic segmentation is focused on your customers' personalities and interests. Here, you should look at customers and define them by their:

- Personality traits
- Hobbies
- Life goals
- Values
- Beliefs
- Lifestyles

Compared to demographic segmentation, this can be a harder set to identify. Good research is vital and, when done well, psychographic segmentation can result in incredibly effective marketing that customers will feel speaks to them on a much more personal level.

Understanding the role your product plays in their life is important too. And this may change with time. You could segment your customers based on their role, for example:

Casual customers: these customers use your product occasionally, but it doesn't play a major role in their lives, nor do they give much thought to its purchase.

Motivated customers: customers of this type are highly motivated to use your service and consider it a significant factor in their lives.

Lifestyle-focused customers: these customers associate your product with the lifestyle they lead or, more importantly, would like to lead.

Know how they buy (Behaviour)

Behavioural segmentation is possibly the most useful of all for startups. As with psychographic segmentation, it requires a fair amount of data to be really effective – however much of it can be collected through your network, website, or app. Here you group customers in respect of their:

- Spending habits
- Purchasing habits
- Browsing habits
- Interactions with your brand
- Loyalty to your brand
- Previous product ratings

To do a good job of profiling and segmenting your customers, perform qualitative, as well as quantitative research, into their characteristics. There are several ways you can do this:

Understand current customers, if you have them, then look at the customers who are most valuable to you. Are there common characteristics?

Use surveys and questionnaires – ask for feedback on how customers use your startup's product or service and what benefits they look for and value. Look at the comments or frequently asked questions (FAQs) on your website and calls – are there common challenges that you resolve for them?

Use social media – the interactive nature of social media gives your team the ability to engage with people and build a picture of your customers.

Now that you know your customers' profile and segmentation, it is time to figure out how they will encounter your startup. You also need a plan for serving and retaining these customers once acquired, as their lifetime value will determine whether acquiring new ones like them is profitable or not.

Determine how best to acquire, serve, and retain them

Selecting and serving the most profitable customers that are right for your startup will be dependent on how good your customer strategy is. Developing a customer strategy is critical to your long-term success and important for shaping your startup's value proposition, offering and capabilities you'll provide to customers, as well as channels that are most effective at delivering those experiences on time with minimal hassle and cost.

You need to create processes that will enable your startup team to learn what your primary customers' values are. You may find you need to do a bit more segmentation based on data analytics, market (and even ethnographic) research, and other methods to reveal needs and preferences that customers themselves may not even be aware of.

Allocate appropriate resources for executing the business model for your customer base e.g., low price (Shoprite), local value creation (Nestlé), global standard of excellence (Google), dedicated service relationship (DHL), or expert knowledge (McKinsey), to borrow from the mature corporate world.

Build an interactive control process with a dashboard to monitor shifts in the assumptions that underlie your choices and prepare an action plan to respond as they occur.

Know how profitable each customer is/will be

I agree with Marc Adresien that getting the right product/market fit (PMF) is critical to a startup's success, and the lack thereof is the primary cause of startup failure, but I don't agree it's the only thing that matters.

Some startups fail after finding PMF because they can't acquire customers who provide profitable margins, leaving them without any chance of success. As such, it became clear to me how crucial acquiring profitable customers is to startup success!

I would go as far as to posit that overpriced customer acquisition is the second biggest cause of startup failure! So, in addition to the classic team, product, and market, you need to add a fourth core element for your startup, a business model that balances the cost of getting customers with your ability to monetise them.

Customer Acquisition Cost (CAC) is your best approximation of the total cost of acquiring a new customer and Lifetime Value (LTV) is an estimate of the average revenue that a customer will generate throughout their lifespan with your startup as a customer. Your CAC is calculated by totalling up your total marketing and sales expenses including salaries and other related expenses over the period in question. You then simply divide that total expense by how many new customers were acquired in that same time frame.

The LTV is a measure of how much profit you can make from one customer over their lifetime. Be aware, the gross margin calculation should take into consideration any installation, maintenance and servicing support costs associated with them as well! A balance between the cost of acquiring customers and your ability to monetise them is necessary for a successful startup business. As I said earlier, CAC exceeding LTV leads to startup failures and a well-balanced business model requires that CAC be significantly less than LTV for customer profitability.

Business models that suffer from an imbalance, such as being unable or unwilling to provide enough value from what you charge will inevitably fail because there's no point in investing time or money in something if it's not going to yield returns.

Question topics you can expect from investors on your customers...

- How well do you know your customer base?

- Where do they live? (Geographic)

- Who are they? (Demographic)

- Why do they buy? (Psychographic)

- How do they buy? (Behavioural)

- How do/will you acquire, serve and retain them?

- How profitable is/will the lifetime value created by each customer acquired be?

CHAPTER 5

Have a valuable product/service offer!

Know your product/service lifecycle!

The basis for any good product, when building startups, revolves around an intrinsic and detailed understanding of your customers, which is then used to develop your products.

A sure way to win your startup's frantic race against time in building a solution for the problem you are trying to solve is not to hope for a lightbulb moment when the product shows up in your head, but to use a methodical, iterative, experimental process. With ever-changing customer needs, lean resources, and variable market events, no product provides endless profitability and all products that rise also eventually fall. This cycle from rise to fall is the product life cycle.

As a founder, it is important that you understand the journey all products take from their development to eventual decline and how to apply it to all your products in order to make more informed decisions that maximise returns. There are five stages that make up every product life cycle with the different durations of each stage giving each product its own unique product life cycle curve. They are:

The product development stage, which is a combination of research, ideation, testing, analysis and bringing your minimum viable product (MVP) into existence for your first set of customers.

Post MVP, your product is introduced to the market, by which time you need a marketing strategy that gets you product-market fit (PMF) with your target customers buying, using, and telling others about your product in numbers large enough to sustain its growth and profitability. Products that find PMF then move into the growth stage, typically scaling from city to country, country to region, or region to global. Marketing at this stage becomes a mission-critical resource.

As the product reaches maturity, growth slows when new or substitute products take centre stage for customers. This is a critical stage for your management and operations to decide on an end-of-life strategy. The final stage is decline, which all products must eventually face and is one of the reasons the development stage must be an ongoing process for your startup. It is important that you recognise which stage of the cycle your product is in so you can use the right approach for extending its life and successfully moving into the next.

It is also important to remember that there isn't a set formula for building products. Building with the customer in mind and understanding your target market are key aspects of this process, but it's also crucial not to neglect decisions about which features or functions will best serve those who buy from you, such as when techies often focus too much time on code instead! To create a great product, you must understand its purpose and why it matters. The more time you spend on this process in the early stages of your startup journey, the better results you will get as you go along!

When creating your product offer, it is worthwhile connecting with the target audience at aspirational and need-based levels. The message should also be simple, direct, and relatable so that potential customers can easily understand what you are offering in just one or two sentences. This will make them more inclined to buy from you instead of someone else who seems an easier option because they're not having to go through all these steps while trying to figure out if there's anything worth investing time/money in!

The most successful startups are those that grow based on word of mouth. As such, marketing and sales budgets are then largely redirected to product development with a focus on customer experience, rather than just doing something better or cheaper. The best use for your startup's products/services is often determined by what customers want, which means, as I said earlier, you should always ask them!

The key to building a successful product is communication with and understanding your customers. Conduct surveys and interviews to gather insights from them about what they want and how they feel about which product features might work best for them.

Take the time to really think about your solution as a product and how it compares to what's already available to your customers. Do some research and try out other products and services that are available to your customers before building your own - don't copycat but always consider their features when making decisions because no two people have identical needs.

If you followed the activities in the previous chapter, you must have done your customer segmentation and profiling. Now you must learn to listen to your customers! This is the bedrock of any product's success. Your customer base will grow organically, and it should do so, once you have a very good product and a good product experience for your customers.

Design how it works.

"Most people make the mistake of thinking design is what it looks like. People think it's this veneer—that the designers are handed this box and told, make it look good! That's not what we think design is. It's not just what it looks like and feels like. Design is how it works."

[Walker, 2003], Steve Jobs

Product design is a way of presenting information about your product so other people can understand and use it.

It's a skill that can be learned through an iterative, incremental process.

Your goal in product design should be to create a product that does something so natural/special/unique that your customers can't help but talk to their friends about it. You must remember that design is the product and must be part of your process from day one. There are five principles of user-centred design you should consider incorporating into your process:

User stories

User stories are short descriptions from a user perspective of what you're building that answer three questions:

- Who's using the product?

- What are they trying to do?

- Why do they need it?

Personas: As explained earlier, personas are fictional characters that represent real customers of your product segmented by their goals, traits and desires.

Emotional design: The most successful designs share a human element with the user. Any technology-enabled product should always be considerate, responsive, and forgiving.

Simplicity: Simplicity is a universal goal in any product design and all good designers strive to make sure their users have a delightful experience by being able to understand easily how the product works, regardless of how they're engaging with it!

Usability testing: The only way to find out if you've succeeded at making the user's life simple is to conduct usability testing to see how people actually use your product to achieve their specific needs.

Don't rush into features, but rather, think about how you can satisfy customer needs with the least functionality. To understand which features should go into your product, you'll need to create user stories based on the customer personas you've created. These stories should be written in a document that describes how the user deals with their problem using your startup's product. It should also list actions customers should take to reach their end goal.

As we begin to see design thinking become the basis of product design, spending more time with your customers becomes a must-do for any right-thinking startup founder. For instance, you create a new feature, you give it to the customers and say: "Hey! What do you feel about this?" Above all, you know it must be a valid proposition that they can relate to.

Most times, designers try to attach value propositions to products that have been built abroad without really understanding the needs of the customer from an emotional point of view. Understanding whether they can even relate to it or whether it is usable.

The best products are the ones which the users can move through intuitively, where you do not need to say "Hey! Click on this, do that." And they have to call you every minute: "Oh, I can't find this button, how do I do this, how do I do that?" It should be the case that anybody or any customer who gets in touch with your product is able to use it seamlessly.

Obviously, your platform being just functional is a no-brainer, but it should be very usable, very reliable, as much as possible, with no down times. Start with the pilots, and gradually begin to scale it from there.

Your startup's choice of features will depend on the core values of your product and these features must satisfy a simple user journey. It's worth remembering that a product can become a minimum marketable product in the future. So, it is advisable that you keep things simple first and then enhance the product with nice-to-have features as you learn from your customers.

It's important that you keep things to the point, plan features iteratively, and expand your product's capabilities only after customer validation.

Creating a product that is easy to understand and use will make it much more likely for you to succeed. The factors which help in this process are communicating your features clearly, signalling the benefits of using the product (without any hidden agenda), listening carefully while customers talk about their needs on social media sites like Facebook, Instagram or Twitter, etc., then implementing what's important according to their feedback, validated through surveys you conducted about the product, as discussed earlier.

Build the right product

Product development is the first stage in creating a new product for your startup. You need to systematically analyse both the idea itself as well as its market and distribution characteristics, before moving on with steps that will transform this into something profitable! At its core, though, it can be driven either by an initial brainstorming session or through research done after careful consideration of target markets where you plan on selling said product. But no matter how things start out, the process always follows similar patterns.

When you are ready to start the product development process, you don't want any surprises along the way, or else your end result could be less than what was expected and would cost time/money to fix! So, before you get started on creating your startup's product offer, here are some things you should consider...

Is your product something that people actually need and want? If not, then you'll have a hard time getting them interested in buying from the concept alone. But if they are already looking for solutions to their problems or pain points from what currently exists on shelves today, this might just be right up their alley!

Is your startup capable of building the product? Building great products has always been difficult, and now it's even more challenging with the array of digital tools at your disposal. You will need to have enough people with the necessary skills and capabilities to profitably build the product.

You should approach every product development from the perspective of your intended customers.

How do we build a truly innovative product or service?

- **Empathise:** understand your user's needs and insights by actively listening and setting aside previous assumptions or unconscious bias.

- **Define:** apply convergent thinking to the data and frame the problem in human-centred language.

- **Ideate:** having defined the problem, start brainstorming and have fun.

- **Prototype:** review your creative ideas and select one or two solutions you want to pursue.

- **Test:** to modify your prototype before sending it to production.

- **Get it to customers.**

Product distribution is the process of delivering products and services alongside selling them from a manufacturer to a customer. Product Distribution Strategy involves designing an efficient method of disseminating your startup's products or services. The goal is to maximise revenue while retaining loyal customers.

There are three approaches to distribution strategy:

- **Intensive Distribution** is used to penetrate the market as much as possible.

- **Selective Distribution** targets selected outlets in specific locations that are based on the particular product within a market (physical or digital).

- **Exclusive Distribution** includes limited outlets such as special collections and outlets selling premium brands.

Product Distribution Channels and Stages refer to the flow of business starting with the manufacturer and ending with the consumer. Your startup will operate somewhere along this value chain.

There are two distribution channels:

- **Direct channel** involves the producer and the consumer. The producer or the manufacturer is in direct contact.

- **Indirect channel** is the opposite of the direct channel. Intermediates are involved in the sales flow.

There are four stages of product distribution:

- **Stage zero:** sales directly involve the manufacturer and the consumer.

- **Stage one:** involves a single intermediate e.g. a retailer.

- **Stage two:** comprises two or more intermediates e.g., a wholesaler and a retailer.

- **Stage three:** consists of the agent/broker who works on behalf of the company dealing with wholesalers.

On Customer Support:

Startups face a unique set of challenges when it comes to distribution. They often have limited resources and must move quickly to reach new markets. This can make it difficult to provide the level of customer support that is critical to long-term success. When problems arise, customers need to be able to rely on prompt and professional service. This is true even if your startup is still in its early stages of development. In many cases, the first interaction a customer has with your startup will be through customer support. If they encounter challenges that are not promptly resolved, they may take their business elsewhere.

However, not only do complaints and feedback provide valuable insights into how your startup can improve its products and services, but they also offer an opportunity to build strong relationships with your customers. In many cases, the way a company handles customer support can be the difference between success and failure.

When done well, customer support can help build brand loyalty and create long-term customers. It can also encourage customer referrals and positive reviews, which can be essential for attracting new customers. In short, customer support is an essential part of the distribution for your startup and should not be overlooked.

Work your business model

Your business model is your startup's core profit-making plan, which defines the products or services you will sell, your target market, and any expected costs. Whether catering to consumers, small businesses or large corporations, your business model sits at the centre of your entrepreneurial journey with your startup.

Your business model is as much a part of defining your business purpose and structure as your mission statement. All too often, founders planning their startups don't spend enough time thinking about their bottom line.

To turn a great idea into a successful business, you need to have defined and developed a workable business model whereby your startup generates revenue, earns profits, and protects its position in the marketplace.

Hundreds of different business models exist. To begin thinking about which kind of model is right for you, you might take a look at how highly successful founders and startups that inspire you have projected themselves.

Price your product right

It's really easy to sell something for free and below cost, so when I am investing in startup companies, I look for a product that is priced at a premium in the marketplace and is driving usage and adoption onto the platform.

Why? Because that means that you've actually hit on a hidden pain point in the marketplace that allows you to charge more than any other offering out there because you are providing the best solution. And in every industry, everywhere, people will pay more if you make their lives easier.

Free is not a pricing strategy, nor is it the bottom line. It may be a good way to get users onto the platform so that you can get feedback and iterate, but that's all. Although it is an excellent tactic, I've often used it to get early adopters onto the platform, to pour information back into the product funnel, so that we understand where we need to change course and, ultimately, how we can solve our needs better. But once you've nailed the problem and you know that you have a minimally viable sellable solution and can get to the first sale, you have to price it! Get rid of the free offering and switch to a paid offering!

Many business operators are averse to showing the price upfront in an offer, worrying that this may reduce the number of interests or leads they receive. Putting the price upfront is to create immediate tension between the value of your offer and the cost of acquiring it.

Assuming the value of your offer is a good one, the price serves to filter away customers you probably don't want anyway, since they are not interested enough to click through and get in touch with you. It saves you the time and hassle of dealing with them and still getting turned down.

Stating the price upfront also puts the onus on the potential customers to internalise and rationalise your offer against their own needs and desires, saving you the trouble of convincing them yourself.

ORGANISATION

The O of POEM is for your startup's business Organisation of the resources that will deliver on the promise of your market Proposition.

Your organisation starts with how you intend to create the startup company legally, beginning with ownership and corporate governance. While there are numerous options available (e.g., sole ownership, partnership, co-operative, etc.), for the purposes for which I write, the most effective legal form for enterprise in most markets is a limited liability company. It provides the visionary entrepreneur (You), your co-founder(s) and other shareholders with a vehicle that is purpose-built for business, provided you document the nature of your relationship appropriately.

Similarly, you need to think through the human value-creation chain (or DNA helix strand) of your business. This means addressing the relationship you envision between the shareholding owners and members of your Board of Directors/Advisers, as well as strategic issues such as executive management roles and responsibilities, and staff conditions of employment.

Next is to work out and be sure to document how the business will function from a process and procedures standpoint. At the minimum, you should be able to describe the buy-side (i.e. procurement, vendor management, etc.), the inside (i.e. human capital, design, development, production, etc.) and the sell-side (i.e. marketing, sales, customer relations, etc.) of your operations.

It is important to demonstrate your mastery (or, as appropriate, lack of knowledge) of your envisioned (or semi-built) organisation in anticipation of helping potential investors, partners, and employees understand how you see it all working operationally to deliver your proposition.

Research, think through and get advice, if need be, to bring to life on paper just how you expect your startup business to work, highlighting key roles and responsibilities of the different units that will make up the company. You should also (if possible) identify the main activities that will make up the daily operations of the business and any issues associated with them that you foresee.

Your approach to addressing corporate policies on matters such as asset acquisition, employee remuneration and customer retention will help or hinder your progress in bringing your vision to life, so be sure to research, discuss, consider, and document your startup company's position on these and any other strategic issues that will give your organisation competitive advantage.

I cannot over-emphasise the value of spending the time to think through, find knowledgeable people to discuss with and address the matters I have raised in this lesson in a document. Recognise that the reality will by necessity be different, thereby subjecting it to constant change.

Taking the time out to go through this thought process concerning your organisation, iterating various components to reflect the development of your thinking and the growth of your startup company, will provide you with a guide for successfully delivering on the promise of your market Proposition.

CHAPTER 6

Build a great team!

It starts with the owners

Owners are the people who control the startup and show up on the Cap Table.

It is not always the case that the owners actually run the company. You've got to decide who owns what and you need to study rights and privileges. If, by now you don't understand them, you really need to sit down, study and understand what should be in a co-founder's statement. Let's talk about how you get one in place, but you really should have one in place already that looks at not just: "Oh, I own ten percent, and you own fifteen percent."

How did you come by those numbers and how do you then ensure that they are on the books, because it's one thing to say we own fifteen percent each; that needs to be documented along with the value you've brought to exchange to do that, and what kind of rights do you have? Is it that we're 50-50, or does somebody have to have 60 percent to be able to take a major decision? Who has the right to sell the company? Is it everybody or nobody? Again, these are things you need to think about when you consider ownership. A few others include:

What you should know about owners as you begin your startup journey:

- Who are the owners of your startup company?

- How much of the company does each owner possess?

- How do you determine co-founders' shareholdings?

- What rights and privileges does each owner have?

- Who has a right to put somebody on the board of directors?

- How much does a person need to own, to put someone else on the board of directors?

Run day-to-day operations well

The Management are the People who run the startup venture.

Looking at who actually runs the company. What are the roles and responsibilities of those running the company?

What do they do on a daily basis? How are you sure they're creating value? Who's on the management team, and who's just a manager? Do you have the right people in your management team? Or is the CTO the one who's doing the marketing? Is it the CEO or the CMO who's coding?

For a startup to be successful, it must be managed effectively. The people in charge of running the company need to have the right skills and knowledge to make sure the business is profitable and grows in the right direction.

The roles and responsibilities of those managing a startup can vary depending on the company's size and stage of development. Generally, the management team is responsible for setting the strategic direction of the business, making sure it stays on track and allocating resources efficiently. They also need to be able to make tough decisions when needed and manage risk effectively.

There are a few key competences that are required to run a company effectively: good communication, leadership skills, strategic thinking, financial literacy, and the ability to make quick decisions. The founding team should also have a clear vision for the startup and be able to inspire the rest of the team to work towards that goal.

The backgrounds and profiles of those in charge of a startup can vary greatly. The management team must be composed of a diverse range of individuals with the appropriate skills and experience. This will help ensure that the company can navigate through different challenges and achieve profitability.

To be successful, it's critical for startups to have a strong management team in place. The right people in charge can make all the difference for any young business, especially a startup.

Find the right people

Employees are the people who work in the startup venture.

In the earliest stages, the people in your startup are the most valuable asset. If you're approaching an Angel or seed investor with just an idea or a prototype and a vision with no validation or customers, they will want to make sure your team is equipped with the necessary experience, expertise, and passion to successfully execute your plan and turn it into the expected outcome. Fundraising is a major reason why starting with a team is important.

A startup needs a leader, builder, and marketer. The leader identifies opportunities, sets a plan, builds a team, and executes. The builder is the creator of the solution, while the marketer brings and boosts sales. Each one of these three roles requires a unique skill and input to shape the overall venture.

It may sound more logical to hire as needed. In other words, when you know what to build, you hire a builder. And when you have what you need to market, you hire a marketer. The truth is, these two roles play a large part in figuring out what to build and market.

They each uniquely evaluate and translate customer insights into actionable plans based on their respective backgrounds and experiences. Developing and marketing your startup concept the right way is another reason why starting with a team is important.

If you're a budget-sensitive founder for whom hiring a builder and marketer from day one is not an option, consider involving and paying them for a startup validation stage, during which they get to contribute to customer development and planning by joining customer interview meetings, investor pitches, sales meetings, and brainstorming sessions. Best of all, this validation stage will serve as a team evaluation period in which to consider the detrimental business and financial consequences of hiring the wrong team members.

Here's where to find and hire an exceptional team:

Specialised Marketplaces

There are many online marketplaces with talented people. A specialised marketplace is different because it chooses and focuses on one specific skill. For instance, many specialised marketing marketplaces filter through thousands of applicants to select and connect you with the best of the best in marketing.

Nowadays, there are specialised marketplaces in development, design, finance, virtual assistance, content creation, and more. If you need assistance finding, interviewing, and hiring the right person, consider using these marketplaces.

Cold Outreach

This feels like a limiting and time-consuming option. But for me, it is how I recruited most of my team members. Sometimes, your ideal team member is only one search away. If you know who you are looking for, don't underestimate the power of search engines and social media research.

Recommendations And Referrals

What is the first thing that comes to mind when you hear someone's recommendation and referral? We usually think about asking someone if they could point us to a talented candidate they worked with and trust. This is only one way you could reach the best team members.

In today's social culture, recommendations and referrals have changed. Think about the last time you saw a social media post by an entrepreneur looking to fill a position. Most of these post types tend to go viral because chances are even if your friends, followers, and group members don't fit the role or are not interested, many would know someone who does. And the post goes viral.

You want to boost the reach of your announcement? Don't hesitate to use cold outreach to contact and ask influencers in the space to spread the word. This is a good question because it is something they can use to help their followers.

In conclusion, before you know it, your startup will no longer be able to operate as a single-person venture and will need the support, skills and expertise of exceptional team members who can help you realise your vision. The sooner you make this investment, the better.

As you begin your startup journey, it's important to think about the talent you will need to help you grow and succeed. What kind of people should you employ? What will their roles and responsibilities be? Who does what for our startup company?

At a startup, every employee has an important role to play. There is no one-size-fits-all answer to this question, as the structure and reporting will vary, depending on the size and stage of your startup. However, in general, you will need a mix of talent and skill sets to help your business thrive.

Your employees can be divided into three main categories:

- **Executives/Management:** these are the senior-level employees who make strategic decisions and oversee day-to-day operations. They may have titles such as CEO, COO, CTO, etc.

- **Functional/Specialist Employees:** these are employees who are experts in a particular area, such as marketing, accounting, or engineering.

- **Entry-Level Employees:** these are employees who are just starting their careers and may have little or no experience of working in a startup.

What are the roles and responsibilities of employees in a startup? Again, this will vary depending on the stage and size of your startup. However, in general, executives/management are responsible for making strategic decisions, while functional/specialist employees are responsible for executing those decisions. Entry-level employees may have a range of responsibilities, depending on their role and the needs of the company.

How do you decide how many employees to hire as a startup? This again depends on the stage and size of your startup. A good rule of thumb is to hire enough employees to get the work done, but not so many that you are bogged down by overhead costs. It's also important to consider the talent pool in your area and how much you can afford to pay your employees.

There are several other factors in addition to the stage of your startup, including your budget and the talent pool in your area. However, in general, you will need a mix of talent and skill sets to help your business succeed.

Partner strategically

Your startup can't do everything by itself, so you're going to need to work with partners who can do what you cannot do. Strategic partners are the organisations and companies that specialise operating in areas that complement your startup's offering, helping you and your team focus on your core capabilities.

To engage with them, you will need to determine what exactly you need external help with. Is it logistics? Marketing? Business development? What?

Once identified, the next step is to determine which organisations are best placed to provide the services you require, noting that: "Oh, as we can't afford to hire an accountant or lawyer right now, do you know of anyone who provides those services to startups?" is one of the most repeated questions I get from early-stage founders.

It is important to have a lawyer on your payroll, even if part-time, or a law firm that's looking after your startup's interests. And the same applies to accounting and finance. If you don't have those two areas professionally managed right from the word go, your startup is not going to last long in business. That can be guaranteed one hundred percent.

Even if you are a lawyer or accountant, you still need those external eyes assessing your startup's operational performance dispassionately and objectively, to give you critically informed views that can only aid your journey to success.

What you should ensure you know about Partners as you progress on your startup journey is...

- What do you need help with in your operations?
- What do you need help with in other activities?
- Which organisations and companies should you partner with?
- What can they do for your startup?
- Why should you partner with them?

Engender a culture of trust and action

In order to attract and retain top talent, startups should always share their mission and values, build an employee-focused culture, involve them in recruiting, get out and meet people and connect online. This is how the people in the startup can work together. It is very important that your startup really knows how to find great talent.

Now that you've found them, how do you actually manage to keep them and what kind of things should you do internally in terms of a working environment? If you don't have an open environment and if people can't ask questions, you won't be able to sustain innovation. If people aren't confident in sharing their ideas, then you know you probably have the wrong culture to sustain innovation.

As a startup, you need curious people who have open minds for you to work with, who know what they are doing, and who are self-motivated. These are critical components that you have to factor in inserting into your culture

What should you know about Culture as you start your startup journey?

When it comes to startups, finding and managing great talent is essential for success. But what do you do if you don't have the budget to offer competitive salaries? How do you keep your top talent from being poached by larger companies? And how can you create a positive working environment that will attract and motivate the best employees?

Here are a few tips on attracting and retaining great talent for your startup:

Cultivate a strong culture.

Your culture is one of the most important factors in attracting and retaining top talent. Make sure your company values are clearly articulated and that employees feel as though they are part of something larger than themselves. Here are some more tips on how to find, manage, and keep great talent for your startup:

- **Promote culture:** a strong culture is one of the biggest attractions for top talent. Make sure your company culture is something that employees can be proud of and that it reflects the values of your startup.

- **Offer growth opportunities:** top talent wants to know that they have a chance to grow and develop their skills. Make sure you offer plenty of opportunities for learning and growth, both professionally and personally.

- **Create a positive work environment:** a happy and productive workforce is crucial to the success of any startup. Make sure your employees feel supported and encouraged to do their best work.

- **Reward excellence:** recognise and reward your top performers for their hard work and dedication. This will help to keep them motivated and engaged.

- **Don't be afraid to invest in talent:** sometimes you have to spend money to make money. If you want to attract and retain the best talent, you may need to offer competitive salaries and benefits.

By following these tips, you can create an environment in which top talent will want to stay and help your startup grow.

CHAPTER 7

Know how to get things done.

Organising, like planning, must be a carefully worked out and applied process. This involves determining what work is needed to accomplish your startup's goal, assigning those tasks to individuals and teams, and arranging them in a decision-making framework (organisational structure).

The end result of your startup's organisational design process should be an organisation wholly consisting of unified parts acting in harmony to execute the tasks required to achieve your startup's goals effectively and efficiently.

A properly implemented organisational process should result in a work environment where all your team members are aware of their responsibilities. If your process is not well executed, it could result in confusion, frustration, loss of efficiency and limited effectiveness.

Evolve a structure that works for your startup

Your organisational structure is how the different units and people in your startup relate to one another, who reports to whom and how people are grouped together to accomplish work. When you begin, your startup is a small business and as such, doesn't need a complex organisational structure. However, you should still take the time to define your company's structure and detail your ownership structure. This will help to ensure that your business runs smoothly.

With the right structure, your company can thrive and grow. The key is finding that delicate balance between hierarchy vs democracy. You want everyone involved in making decisions on what needs to be done next. It is important to remember that profitability is key when it comes to startups, so make sure that you put measures in place to ensure that your business is making a profit.

In addition, you should also create a management and operational structure chart of your startup. This will help to ensure that your business runs smoothly and that all key aspects are being managed effectively.

Creating a well-defined organisational structure is essential for any startup. By taking the time to define your company's structure, you can ensure that your business will be profitable and efficient.

Governance is critical to decision making

Governance may be defined as: "The system by which entities are directed and controlled. It is concerned with structure and processes for decision-making, accountability, control, and behaviour at the top of an entity. Governance influences how an organisation's objectives are set and achieved, how risk is monitored and addressed and how performance is optimised". In this case, that "entity" is your startup.

Proper governance will ensure that everyone in your startup follows appropriate and transparent decision-making processes and that the interests of all your stakeholders (owners, managers, employees, partners, customers, and others) are duly protected.

Governance provides you with a clear distinction between the owners of your startup (the shareholders) and the managers (the board of directors) when it comes to making strategic decisions.

A good governance system for your startup should include but not be limited to the following:

- Ensuring that the management of your startup considers the best interests of all stakeholders in decision-making.

- Helping your startup deliver long-term financial growth and economic impact.

- Improving your startup's valuation as it reassures investors that you are a good investment for their money.

- Giving you control of appropriate management and information systems (such as security or risk management).

- Giving guidance to the owners and managers as to the goals and strategies of your startup.

- Minimising opportunities for wastage, corruption, risks, and mismanagement of your startup's resources.

- Helping to create a strong brand reputation for your startup in the market.

- Your startup's performance and the performance of your board.

- The relationship between your board and your startup's management.

- Selection, appointment, and evaluation of your startup's board of directors.

- Your board's (Advisory and Directors) membership and responsibilities.

- Risk management, corporate compliance, and internal controls.

- Communication between your startup's shareholders and management.

- Financial reporting by your startup.

Develop strategies for operational success

An operations strategy is a plan that specifies how your startup will allocate your resources (i.e., money, people, and facilities) to support its product development, marketing, sales, customer management, and other business activities. Your operation's strategy is the sum of the actions your startup intends to take to achieve your long-term goals. Together, these actions make up your startup's strategic plan. Your plans may take some time to complete as you require involvement from all team members.

You need to work as a team to create the operation's strategy to ensure everyone becomes familiar with the goals and objectives being aimed for by your startup. Your operation's strategy should address building the structure of your startup into a form that enables the delivery of your vision for it.

The strategic plan resulting from it must be developed with a vision in mind and address all aspects of your startup's operations. Once in place, all company goals and tactics should revolve around its execution.

- What should we know about Operations Strategy as we begin our startup journey?

- What is our primary competitive advantage and plan for the growth of our startup?

- How do we ensure we stay relevant in our market? How do we leverage free or inexpensive marketing and advertising strategies and tools to create an effective brand design for our startup? (Brand communication).

- How do we identify, acquire, serve, and retain the most profitable customers in the market? (CRM).

Put policies, processes & procedures in place for your operations

Operations are your business's day-to-day organisational activities that create unique value and achieve core objectives. Operations play distinctive roles that contribute towards the overall success of the organisation. The Merriam-Webster dictionary describes an operation as the "performance of a practical work or something involving the practical application of principles or processes." The scope of operations varies with the type and size of your business.

The term "operations" embraces all the activities required to create and deliver an organisation's goods or services to its customers or clients. The specific definition of operations will depend on your industry and the stage your business is in. Sometimes, improving operations means thinking strategically about your systems and processes. Other times, it means being part of the on-the-ground work to bring every aspect of a project, from tiny to huge, to reality.

Operations are key to running a business that always gets better and better at what it does. By taking a look at how your business is run and asking yourself questions about existing processes, you'll be able to define and optimise what operations mean for you and your business.

What you should know about Organisation Operations as you begin your startup journey:

- What are your production and distribution methods?

- How do you deliver your startup's value proposition? (Distribution)

- Which channels does your startup use to engage with customers? (Communications)

- How do these channels reach your customer segments? (Delivery)

- What are the significant risk factors (e.g., dependence on raw materials or key suppliers or customers) affecting your startup's production capacity and your ability to expand?

Proactively manage partners

A third-party vendor is a person or company that provides services for another company (or that company's customers). While vendors are considered "third parties," some industries differentiate a "third-party vendor" specifically as a vendor under a written contract, but not all vendors work under a contract.

Third-party vendors in the digital world include cloud hosting providers, cloud-based/SaaS software solutions, business partners, suppliers, and agencies. Any person or business that accesses and processes a company's data is also considered a third-party vendor. This can include tax professionals, accountants, consultants, and email list services, among others.

What are some examples of third-party vendor goods and services? Goods and services obtained from third-party vendors can include, but aren't limited to:

- **Cloud web hosting services:** a cloud hosting vendor might provide everything from disk space and bandwidth to encryption and high-tech security solutions.

- **Cloud-based software solutions:** SaaS software vendors provide access to software programs either for your business or your customers. For example, marketing automation platforms, CRMs, accounting packages, etc.

- **Equipment maintenance:** the company that fixes your copy machine and the team that manages your network security are third-party vendors.

- **HVAC servicing:** the local HVAC company that services your unit provides third-party vendor services.

- **Contractors of any kind:** any contractor, short or long-term, is a third-party vendor.

- **Call centre providers:** if you host your call centre with another company, it is considered a third-party vendor.

- **Bookkeeping/financial auditors:** any person or business hired to manage your finances, budget, or audit your finances is a third-party vendor.

- **Lawyers:** sometimes it's necessary to consult a lawyer before signing contracts or making big purchases. All legal services are considered third-party vendors.

What are the risks of using third-party vendors?

If your vendors fail to deliver, you'll fail to deliver. However, risk is inherent in any business relationship. Using third-party vendors comes with many risks, most of which can be mitigated. The biggest risk is choosing a third-party vendor who doesn't align with your security standards. When you're bound by data privacy regulations, you need to know exactly what security standards are being implemented and if your vendors aren't on par with them, you must try to remediate that. Otherwise, you're risking a data breach.

Every vendor you do business with should meet or exceed your company's security standards. You also need to perform security risk assessments periodically to find out where your company is vulnerable, so you can fix those problem areas quickly. Risk assessments can be cumbersome and time-consuming, especially with multiple vendors.

What you should know before hiring a third-party service:

- Clarity of Engagement

- Keep the Timeline in Mind

- Understand the Legal Aspect

- Do Not Share Complete Control

What you should know about the organisation of Third Parties as you begin your startup journey:

- Are responsibilities to manage these risks clearly defined individually for each third-party and as a whole?

- Are we monitoring the various risks and contract requirements associated with each existing relationship and at what interval?

- How do we gain reassurance that information provided by third parties is valid, accurate, and complete?

- Have we inventoried the third-party relationships that exist in our organisation?

- When evaluating new relationships, do our selection criteria address risks to the organisation?

CHAPTER 8

Deploy the right technology.

Create a technology roadmap

Launching a new product is an interesting and exciting process for every startup. So, you have already validated your idea for market fit, raised some seed investments and are ready to embark on this journey? Great! But you don't want to spend half a year of your life without any guarantee of success? Read on to learn the pros and cons of MVP development and how to minimise the duration of this process!

Prolonged MVP development duration is one of the biggest risks you might face. Should you miss the window of opportunity, more agile competitors are sure to take your market share.

MVP stands for Minimum Viable Product, the smallest set of features that can be used to solve some real-world pain of your customers and provide the feedback needed to continue the app development. MVP software development by a remote software development team or technology vendor is the most feasible way for a startup to get the product to the market quickly, with minimal risks and maximum cost-efficiency. Why so?

An MVP helps you get real-world data early to validate users' interest in your product and adjust the feature set based on customers' feedback. In addition, MVP development helps minimise the losses in case the product gains little traction. Thus, MVP development is an essential stage for every startup. However, MVP development requires a skilled team in order to succeed. Hiring a team while developing a product is very risky as it can break the whole project. Therefore, many startups outsource MVP development to a remote team of software engineers. While developing an MVP using a remote team, startups can hire in-house expertise quickly and lay the foundation for further growth.

But how long should the MVP software development take? It depends on the scope of work that must be done, the technology stack, the team availability, the processes' maturity, the degree of customer involvement, and dedication to the project (and the speed of making the executive decisions on the customer side).

There are various methods and practices for minimising the duration and budget of your MVP development. Based on our experience, the shortest time to build an MVP was three months. Why was it done so fast and what contributed to the product becoming a success?

To build an MVP in 3 months or fewer, the following conditions must be met:

- Working with a tech vendor skilled in delivering MVPs quickly. This must be proven by relevant cases and satisfied clients you can contact, not by testimonials and reviews alone.

- Partnering with a CTO or tech advisor able to control the MVP development from a technological and process standpoint.

- A concept validation and market-fit check before MVP development starts.

- An in-depth discovery phase to define the MVP scope and roadmap.

- Two-sided management of the MVP scope. You, as well as the MVP implementation, must secure the MVP scope and make sure it does not grow to include various great ideas and wishes that might come up during the implementation.

Your architecture and development methodology are key (Feedback Loops, Agile and the Lean Startup Model)

Creating a software system is a lot like constructing a building. If the foundations are not solid, structural problems can undermine the integrity and function of the building.

When designing technology solutions on Amazon Web Services (AWS), if you neglect the five pillars of operational excellence, security, reliability, performance efficiency and cost optimization, it can become challenging to build a system that delivers on your expectations and requirements.

Incorporating these pillars into your architecture helps produce stable and efficient systems. This allows you to focus on the other aspects of design, such as functional requirements.

The AWS Well-Architected Framework helps cloud architects build the most secure, high-performing, resilient, and efficient infrastructure possible for their applications. The framework provides a consistent approach for customers and AWS Partner Network (APN) Partners to evaluate architectures and provides guidance to implement designs that scale with your application needs over time.

In this section, we provide an overview of the Well-Architected Framework's five pillars and explore design principles and best practices.

Operational Excellence

The Operational Excellence pillar includes the ability to support development and run workloads effectively, gain insight into their operation, and continuously improve supporting processes and procedures to deliver business value. You can find prescriptive guidance on implementation in the Operational Excellence Pillar whitepaper.

Design Principles for Operational Excellence. There are five design principles for operational excellence in the cloud:

- Perform operations as code

- Make frequent, small, reversible changes

- Refine operations procedures frequently

- Anticipate failure

- Learn from all operational failures

Operations teams need to understand their business and customer needs so they can support business outcomes. Ops create and use procedures to respond to operational events, and validate their effectiveness to support business needs. Ops also collect metrics that are used to measure the achievement of desired business outcomes.

Everything continues to change: your business context, business priorities, customer needs, etc. It's important to design operations to support evolution over time in response to change and to incorporate lessons learned through their performance.

Security:

The Security pillar includes the ability to protect data, systems, and assets to take advantage of cloud technologies to improve your security. You can find prescriptive guidance on implementation in the Security Pillar whitepaper.

Design Principles for Security. There are seven design principles for security in the cloud:

- Implement a strong identity foundation
- Enable traceability
- Apply security at all layers
- Automate security best practises
- Protect data in transit and at rest
- Keep people away from data
- Prepare for security events

Before you design any workload, you need to put in place practices that influence security. You'll want to control who can do what. In addition, you want to be able to identify security incidents, protect your systems and services, and maintain the confidentiality and integrity of data through data protection.

You should have a well-defined and practised process for responding to security incidents. These tools and techniques are important because they support objectives such as preventing financial loss or complying with regulatory obligations.

The AWS Shared Responsibility Model enables organisations that adopt the cloud to achieve their security and compliance goals. Because AWS physically secures the infrastructure that supports your cloud services, as an AWS customer, you can focus on using services to accomplish your goals. The AWS Cloud also provides greater access to security data and an automated approach to responding to security events.

Reliability:

The Reliability pillar encompasses the ability of a workload to perform its intended function correctly and consistently when it's expected to. This includes the ability to operate and test the workload through its total lifecycle. You can find prescriptive guidance on implementation in the Reliability Pillar whitepaper.

Design Principles for Reliability. There are five design principles for reliability in the cloud:

- Automatically recover from failure

- Test recovery procedures

- Scale horizontally to increase aggregate workload availability

- Stop guessing capacity

- Manage change in automation

To achieve reliability, you must start with the foundations, an environment where service quotas and network topology accommodate the workload. The workload architecture of the distributed system must be designed to prevent and mitigate failures. The workload must handle changes in demand or requirements, and it must be designed to detect failure and automatically heal itself.

Before designing any system, foundational requirements that influence reliability should be in place. For example, you must have sufficient network bandwidth for your data centre. These requirements are sometimes neglected (because they are beyond a single project's scope).

This neglect can have a significant impact on the ability to deliver a reliable system. In an on-premises environment, these requirements can cause long lead times due to dependencies and, therefore, must be incorporated during initial planning.

With AWS, most of these foundational requirements are already incorporated or may be addressed as needed. The cloud is designed to be essentially limitless, so it is the responsibility of AWS to satisfy the requirement for sufficient networking and computer capacity, while you are free to change resource size and allocation, such as the size of storage devices, on demand.

Performance Efficiency:

The Performance Efficiency pillar includes the ability to use computing resources efficiently to meet system requirements and to maintain that efficiency as demand changes and technologies evolve. You can find prescriptive guidance on implementation in the Performance Efficiency Pillar whitepaper.

Design Principles for Performance Efficiency. There are five design principles for performance efficiency in the cloud:

- Democratise advanced technologies

- Go global in minutes

- Use serverless architectures

- Experiment more often

- Consider mechanical sympathy

Take a data-driven approach to building a high-performance architecture. Gather data on all aspects of the architecture, from the high-level design to the selection and configuration of resource types.

Reviewing your choices on a regular basis ensures you are taking advantage of the continually evolving AWS Cloud. Monitoring ensures you are aware of any deviance from expected performance. Make trade-offs in your architecture to improve performance, such as using compression or caching, or relaxing consistency requirements.

The optimal solution for a particular workload varies and solutions often combine multiple approaches. Well-designed workloads use multiple solutions and enable different features to improve performance.

Cost Optimization:

The Cost Optimization pillar includes the ability to run systems to deliver business value at the lowest price point. You can find prescriptive guidance on implementation in the Cost Optimization Pillar whitepaper.

Design Principles for Cost Optimization. There are five design principles for cost optimization in the cloud:

- Implement cloud financial management

- Adopt a consumption model

- Measure overall efficiency

- Stop spending money on undifferentiated heavy lifting

- Analyse and attribute expenditure

As with the other pillars, there are trade-offs to consider. For example, do you want to optimise for speed to market or for cost? In some cases, it's best to optimise for speed: going to market quickly, shipping new features, or simply meeting a deadline, rather than investing in up-front cost optimisation.

Design decisions are sometimes driven by haste rather than data, and there is always the temptation to overcompensate rather than spend time benchmarking for the most cost-optimal deployment. This might lead to over-provisioned and under-optimised deployments.

Using the appropriate services, resources and configurations for your workloads are key to cost savings.

Build, measure, learn...

A core component of Lean Startup methodology is the build-measure-learn feedback loop. The first step is figuring out the problem that needs to be solved and then developing a minimum viable product (MVP) to begin the process of learning as quickly as possible. Once the MVP is established, a startup can work on tuning the engine. This will involve measurement and learning and must include actionable metrics that can demonstrate cause and effect questions.

The startup will also utilise an investigative development method called the "Five Whys", asking simple questions to study and solve problems along the way. When this process of measuring and learning is done correctly, it will be clear that a company is either moving the drivers of the business model or not. If not, it is a sign that it is time to pivot or make a structural course correction to test a new fundamental hypothesis about the product, strategy, and engine of growth.

Build-Measure-Learn may sound simplistic, but it's been a game-changing technique for businesses that previously developed products without getting potential customers' input. Sometimes, companies would get lucky, but many wound up making sophisticated products that no one wanted.

Build-Measure-Learn improves on the "just do it" approach with an incremental, iterative methodology that replaces assumption with knowledge and certainty.

Using the Model

Follow these steps to work through a Build-Measure-Learn feedback loop:

Step 1: Plan

The model may be called "Build-Measure-Learn" but, if you follow that sequence and jump in at the "Build" phase, you'll be missing the mark. Instead, it's essential to start with a planning stage.

Your first task is to define the idea that you want to test and the information that you need to learn. You do this by developing a hypothesis: your prediction of what will happen during the experiment.

Your hypothesis could focus on anything from product features and customer service ideas to finding the best pricing strategies and distribution channels. You might, for example, hypothesise that "increasing the frequency of our newsletters from two to four per month will increase overall revenue."

Next, decide what you'll need to measure to test your hypothesis, and plan how you'll collect your data. Interviews, surveys, website analytics, and specialised software programs are common methods for gathering data, and the BADIR process will help you to structure your study.

Step 2: Build

Your goal here is to create a Minimum Viable Product (MVP): the smallest possible product that allows you to test your hypothesis.

It could be a working prototype or a basic advertisement or landing page. It could be a presentation slideshow, a mock brochure, a sample dataset, a storyboard, or a video that illustrates what you offer. Whatever MVP you choose, it needs to show just enough core features to attract the interest of early adopters; the people who'll likely want to buy your product as soon as it launches.

For example, the first 5,000 people who subscribed to the cloud-based file sharing company Dropbox™ did so before its service was launched. They'd been convinced by the strength of Dropbox's MVP: a 90-second video explaining the service that it was about to offer.

Step 3: Measure

Here, you measure the results that you obtained in Step 2. How does what actually happened compare with your hypothesis? Is there sufficient interest in your idea to continue developing it? Does the data show that you'll be able to build a sustainable business around your product or service?

Step 4: Learn

By the time you reach this stage, you'll be equipped to make sound, evidence-based business decisions about what to do next.

There are then two ways forward:

Persevere:

Your hypothesis was correct, so you decide to press on with the same goals. You repeat the feedback loop to continuously improve and refine your idea. (Even though your idea has achieved sufficient initial success to persevere with it, bear in mind that your next iteration may not do so. Be prepared to pivot in the future.)

Pivot:

The experiment has refuted your hypothesis, but you've still gained valuable knowledge about what doesn't work. You can reset, or correct your course and repeat the loop, using what you've learned to test new hypotheses and carry out different experiments. You can pivot in various ways. For example, you could develop a single feature from your MVP (called "zoom-in pivoting") or focus on a different type of customer ("customer segment pivoting"). Or, you could try delivering through a new channel ("channel pivoting",) or use a single feature as the basis of a different product ("zoom-out pivoting").

ECONOMICS

Economics are the measures of the startup's use of available capital for funding expenses that generate impact...

How does the startup team plan for the future when there is no certainty about what that future will look like? What methods and tools does it use for cash flow management? How does the startup meet financial challenges and plan for an unpredictable future as economic and business pressures take their toll? How does it advance one or more of the United Nations Sustainable Development Goals (SDGs)?

These are some of the questions considered as part of the economics of any Startup using the POEM Framework.

Capital—Equity, Grants, Prizes, Cash...

The economic journey of a start-up begins with capital both human and financial. Financial capital is what the founders raise to pay for any or all of the required expenses involved in creating their new business. The first capital to come into the company is typically the founder's human capital which is often accompanied by financial capital in the form of cash, grants, and sometimes, loans. Family, Friends, Fans (and some say Fools), aka FFF, usually contribute the first capital raised by the startup in the form of cash and/or time spent as "Sweat Equity", becoming the first shareholders aside from the founders. In addition to the cash and loans from FFF, there may also be grants and prizes along the way, given startups are built on innovation.

The first external source of capital for mature startup ecosystems on the continent, such as those of Cairo, Lagos, Nairobi, Johannesburg and Cape Town, are business angels who provide startups with small amounts of cash typically from $5,000 individually and up to $250,000 or more as syndicates and networks. In addition to cash as equity, convertible debt or increasingly SAFE (simple agreement for future equity), they provide mentoring and advice to the founders they invest in, as well as access to their business networks.

As the startup grows and its need for capital increases, early stage Venture Capital (VC) invest in Seed rounds that ignite the growth and scaling of the startup and, if things go to plan, Series A, B and on to the later stages with VCs and even Private Equity (PE) firms, when the needs become significant and the way to sustainability is clear.

Expenses—Costs, Burn Rate, Liabilities...

Capital is the lifeblood of a startup, but expenses are the fuel that fires the income engine. Expenses are the continuous stream of costs associated with the startup's activities from launch through to sustainability. In the beginning, this includes paying for founding employees, acquiring office space and equipment, procuring any licences or permits needed, buying inventory, conducting or procuring market and other research, market testing, product development, marketing, sales and other launch-related expenses.

Once launched, the burn rate is used by startups (and investors) to track the amount of monthly cash that the startup spends before it starts generating its own income. A startup's burn rate is also used as a measuring stick for its runway, the amount of time it has before it runs out of money. Gross burn is the total amount of operating costs it racks up each month, while the net burn is the total amount of money it loses monthly.

Getting a tech startup from an idea to a minimum viable product (MVP) will usually involve a peculiar set of expenses. The biggest expense a tech startup has, in the beginning, is the app development and design. If it has a technical co-founder with a programming background, instead of cash, the investment will represent time spent building the product (human capital). It is worth noting here that the two most critical factors in tech startup product development expenses are the complexity of the app and developer rates.

Increasingly, startups are having to rely on paid marketing acquisition channels such as social media and search engine advertising for growth, making marketing an expense to cater for. The cost of incorporating a startup depends on the jurisdiction and legal structure but is an expense that must be borne early in the process too. The website domain name (a premium domain name can be expensive), hosting and cloud storage expenses must also be considered.

Other expenses that should be budgeted for include accounting, legal (especially if operating in highly regulated sectors), transaction fees (banks and professional service providers), travel, transportation, memberships, and other fees. Food for thought is the expense of making the wrong decisions in recruiting employees, developing the product/service offer and even marketing. As a rule, reserve at least a quarter of your initial investment to cover these kinds of expenses.

Impact—Income + SDG...

Profitable income at scale remains the holy grail for startups. Investors prefer to see revenue growth instead of profit because they know that the margin between income and profit can be carved from efficiencies that are uncovered in growth. Once scale and efficiency drive the price down, profit appears. The IFRS (International Financial Reporting Standards) are clear on financial reporting with the bottom line being the last line in an income statement that gives the startup's net profit (i.e. how profitable it's been recently (usually quarterly or annually) after all expenses have been accounted for.)

When it comes to the impact any product/service offering is having in the market, growth is the simplest measure. Growth in customers, revenue, profit, SDG achievements, assets, employees, and the list goes on. Given that the value exchange with customers has a direct impact (e.g. carbon savings) or results in impact (e.g. literacy), then a hard measure of impact is the growth of the customer base and, by implication, the growth in revenue and usually associated expenses.

The generation of revenue is tied to customer segments and their continual stream of customer-desired features being delivered in the product/service offering. Customer acquisition becomes the focal point of most startups at this stage, with that focus shifting to retention as they find Product Market Fit and begin the journey to Channel Product Fit. Then as startups scale up, they realise the 80/20 rule of the customer base and methods like key account management kick in to drive revenue to sustainability.

All this while keeping a keen eye on taxation as the startup's social responsibility as a good corporate citizen. As an ardent fan of the IFRS reporting standards (which is a reason an accountant on the startup team is a must-have), the economics is actually a superset of the accounting methods they lay out, as it also embraces the UN standards for reporting on the Sustainable Development Goals (SDG).

That perpetual balancing act between capital, expenses, income, and impact is the economic dance of the startup founder as they develop the African continent.

Long may they dance!

CHAPTER 9

Make sure the funding is sufficient.

C apital is the money your business has or needs to run its day-to-day operations, fund, and grow your startup. It's a means to an end, not an end in itself. The end goal is to build a product, a community, and a profitable business.

Fundraising is the seeking and gathering of financial contributions to help you build a successful business, by engaging family, friends, angel investors, and venture partners. Raising money is time-consuming. It requires creative energy and can drag on a lot longer than planned.

Getting a 'yes' can sometimes take up to six months while getting a 'no' can sometimes take longer. Have multiple sources of capital for your startup.

It is important that you ask yourself "what is the best option for me and my business at this time?", in the phase of your development

- Your Personal Savings
- Loans (Secured & Unsecured)
- Family and Friends
- Accelerators
- Customers
- Bootstrapping
- Angel Investors
- Grants
- Venture Capitalists
- Competitions
- Crowdfunding Fans

Know what to look for in investors and how to manage them

- **People:** who are they, what is their reputation, and track record?

- **Portfolio/Resource:** a good balance of resources to startups, will they be able to help you or will you be lost in the portfolio?

- **Specialisation and focus:** common area of focus, area of interest, smart money, support of your business, ask about past investments.

- **Follow-on policy:** a good investor/VC should have a well-communicated follow-on investment policy to support in later rounds of funding.

- **Values:** code of conduct, word on the street, agreements, fairness to founders.

- **Resources and sources:** does the investor have easy connections, access, or a platform that provides services, i.e. legal, regulations, PR, marketing, and branding?

Start growing your investor network before you even need to raise funding.

- Cold email.

- Pre-record your Canva presentation to present anytime, anywhere.

- The update email.

- Add audio or record yourself talking over a presentation.

- Follow-on Funding

- You will likely need follow-on investments. Ideally, you want current investors to come on board in the next round of fundraising.

- Investors provide access to a network of experienced operators.

- Investors bring a wealth of knowledge and experience.

- Angel investors have a pipeline of great talent and can help with scouting.
- Create a simple reporting template
  - Data and Metrics
  - Burn rate
  - Financial overview
  - Cash in hand
  - Highlights
  - Customer growth
  - Lowlights
  - Talent
  - Challenges

Examples of Investor reports

We have some problems with [Product Initiative]. We are lacking experience in [X]. Can you recommend a [Mentor/Partner/etc.] to come in and help (this can be a paid coaching position)?

I have been approached by a VC who wants to potentially pre-empt a [Series X]. How do I best deal with this?

I am worried that [key competitor X] has just closed a [$X Round] (see here for more info). How shall we best deal with this (if at all)?

We have lost two important [customers/potential customers] due to [X]. Can any of you spare some time to talk through our positioning statements and sales process?

Fundraising: We are actively raising a series A. My goal is to finalise it by the end of the quarter. Here is the current list of conversations and updates. If there is someone missing, please let me know.

Learnings since the last update.

Be clear at which stage of funding you are, as I said earlier:

- It starts with Pre-Seed funding by FFF.

- Then Seed Stage Funding by Angels and Early VC.

- Growth Stage Funding is a serious VC business.

- Scale-up Funding is the big leagues.

The question is: at which stage of funding is your startup, and do you have the right investors on your cap table?

Use the right tools to raise funding for your startup

- **Develop a Business Plan:** Presentation (Short and long), Financial Plan, Team with a track record, Testimonials from customers, Data from market research, Competitive analysis, and Legal documents.

- **Product launch:** Validation, Traction, Feedback, Customers.

- **Assemble a team of Advisers:** Founders, Investors, Industry Experts, and Influencers.

- **Find founders ahead of you in the process:** Learn from each other. Share stories on progress and get honest feedback.

- **Be prepared:** Understand and know your business, Engage the investor to make sure they are right for you.

- **Track Record:** Investors are looking for a great team. They believe a good team would be successful with a difficult business and pivot to fit the market, while a bad team won't be successful with a business that is easy to expand. Investors love serial entrepreneurs or people with great experiences and a proven track record.

Be clear on which instruments are being used to invest in your startup

Investors will agree to one of the following depending on the stage of the company:

- Convertible notes (simple loan)

- Equity

- SAFE

Match the use of funds by your startup with disbursement by funders:

- To grow the business
- Product development: MVP, Go to Market, Marketing, Talent Working Capital, Asset Purchase, Growth Funding
- Understand and be comfortable with milestones

Know the expected returns, risks, and mitigations.

The money made or lost on an investment over a period of time:

Investing in startups is risky. Every early-stage investor believes they will do 100X even though we all know it's one of the highest-risk asset classes.

- 75-90% of startups fail or fail to scale.
- Most investors get some returns through an exit, dividend, or interest.

Know your startup's capital needs

- How much in US$ do you need to raise right now?
- How much working capital does your startup have?
- How much capital have you raised since you started?

- How much equity has your startup been able to raise?

- Who are your startup's shareholders?

- Does your startup have any debt?

- How much debt does it have?

- Has your startup been able to secure prizes and/or grants for itself?

- Is your startup generating cash flow?

- How much cash does your startup currently have available to carry out its operations?

CHAPTER 10

Make money work for you.

Target which assets your startup owns/acquires

There are two categories for defining assets. The first refers to anything that is in hand when starting out a company. This can be anything valuable such as cash in a bank account, equipment, land, or buildings. It can also refer to other valuable assets such as inventions, software or even trademarks and copyrights.

The second category of assets refers to the items a startup will need when launching. These can be machinery or equipment, or even the raw materials required to build products. It can also include assets such as office buildings or office equipment, such as computers and stationery.

These are known as startup assets. And what is classified as such will vary, depending on what type of business you are launching. The reason why this is important is that these assets are a large part of the cost of getting the business started.

As a founder, calculating these assets is also important, because doing so will affect the amount of funding your startup is able to garner. You need to accurately work out how much money you need for startup assets when looking for funding and must include these in your financial projections.

When doing this, remember that you are making estimates. The figures you come up with do not have to be correct and will probably not be exactly correct anyway. Due to this fact, you should always add about 10-20% to the figure you have estimated, and avoid going into too much depth when working out these numbers.

What you should know about assets as you begin your startup journey.

- What assets do we need to have? How can we ensure the long-term sustainability of these assets?

- How can we identify the risk of an asset-related disaster?

- What can an evaluation of the condition of our critical assets look like?

Know what liabilities your startup has/incurs

In financial accounting, a liability is defined as the future sacrifices of economic benefits that the entity is obliged to make to other entities as a result of past transactions or other past events,[1] the settlement of which may result in the transfer or use of assets, provision of services or other yielding of economic benefits in the future.

A liability is defined by the following characteristics:

- Any type of borrowing from persons or banks for improving a business or personal income that is payable during a short or long term ;

- A duty or responsibility to others that entails settlement by future transfer or use of assets, provision of services, or other transactions yielding an economic benefit, at a specified or determinable date, on the occurrence of a specified event, or on demand;

- A duty or responsibility that obliges the entity to another, leaving it little or no discretion to avoid settlement; and

- A transaction or event obliging the entity that has already occurred.

Liabilities in financial accounting need not be legally enforceable but can be based on equitable obligations or constructive obligations. An equitable obligation is a duty based on ethical or moral considerations.

A constructive obligation is an obligation that is implied by a set of circumstances in a particular situation, as opposed to a contractually based obligation.

The accounting equation relates to assets, liabilities, and owner's equity:

- Assets = Liabilities + Owner's Equity

The accounting equation is the mathematical structure of the balance sheet.

What you should know about Liabilities as you start your startup journey.

- How can we best identify liability risks around our startup?

- What would be the best ways to go about liability insurance for our startup?

- Why should discounts payable on short-term notes be considered liabilities?

Know your expenses, burn rate and how much runway you have

Startup costs are the expenses incurred during the process of creating a new business. All businesses are different, so they require different types of startup costs. Online businesses have different needs than brick-and-mortar; coffee shops have different requirements than bookstores. However, a few expenses are common to most business types.

Common Startup Business Costs

The Business Plan: Essential to the startup effort is creating a business plan, a detailed map of the new business. A business plan forces consideration of the different startup costs. Underestimating expenses falsely increase expected net profit, a situation that does not bode well for any small business owner.

Research Expenses: Careful research of the industry and consumer makeup must be conducted before starting a business. Some business owners choose to hire market research firms to aid them in the assessment process. For business owners who choose to follow this route, the expense of hiring these experts must be included in the business plan.

Borrowing Costs: Starting up any kind of business requires an infusion of capital. There are two ways to acquire capital for a business: equity financing and debt financing. Usually, equity financing entails the issuance of stock, but this does not apply to most small businesses, which are proprietorships.

For small business owners, the most likely source of financing is debt in the form of a small business loan. Business owners can often get loans from banks, savings institutions, and the U.S. Small Business Administration (SBA). Like any other loan, business loans are accompanied by interest payments. These payments must be planned for when starting a business, as the cost of default is very high. For startups, the story is different....

Insurance, Licence and Permit Fees: Many businesses are expected to submit to health inspections and authorisations to obtain certain business licences and permits. Some businesses might require basic licences while others need industry-specific permits. Carrying insurance to cover your employees, customers, business assets, and yourself can help protect your personal assets from any liabilities that may arise.

Technological Expenses: Technological expenses include the cost of a website, information systems and software, including accounting and point of sale (POS) software, for a business. Some small business owners choose to outsource these functions to other companies to save on payroll and benefits.

Equipment and Supplies: Every business requires some form of equipment and basic supplies. Before adding equipment expenses to your list of startup costs, a decision has to be made to lease or buy. The state of your finances will play a major part in this decision. Even if you have money to buy equipment, unavoidable expenses may make leasing, with the intention to buy at a later date, a viable option. However, it is important to remember that, regardless of the cash position, a lease may not always be best, depending upon the type of equipment and terms of the lease.

Advertising and Promotion: A new company or startup business is unlikely to succeed without promoting itself. However, promoting a business entails much more than placing ads in a local newspaper. It also includes marketing: everything a company does to attract clients to the business. Marketing has become such a science that any advantage is beneficial, so external dedicated marketing companies are most often hired.

Employee Expenses: Businesses planning to hire employees must include wages, salaries, and benefits, also known as the cost of labour. Failure to compensate employees adequately can end in low morale, mutiny, and bad publicity, all of which can be disastrous to a company.

What you should know about Expenses as you start your startup journey.

- What will it cost to contract with an accountant or a financial advisor?

- How do we identify costs associated with licensing and permits?

- How do we calculate taxes, and what are the best ways to pay them - quarterly or yearly?

How much revenue are you generating at what growth rate?

Revenue is the value of all sales of goods and services recognised by a company in a period. Revenue (also referred to as Sales or Income) forms the beginning of a company's income statement and is often considered the "Top Line" of a business. Expenses are deducted from a company's revenue to arrive at its Profit or Net Income.

Revenue Model

- Who Pays
- What is paid
- For what is paid
- How are you paid
- How much is paid

Revenue Recognition Principle

According to the revenue recognition principle in accounting, revenue is recorded when the benefits and risks of ownership have transferred from seller to buyer, or when the delivery of services has been completed.

Notice that this definition doesn't include anything about payment for goods/services being received. This is because companies often sell their products on credit to customers, meaning that they won't receive payment until later.

When goods or services are sold on credit, they are recorded as revenue, but since a cash payment is not received yet, the value is also recorded on the balance sheet as accounts receivable.

When the cash payment is finally received later, there is no additional income recorded, but the cash balance goes up, and accounts receivable goes down.

Revenue Example

Below is an example of Amazon's 2017 income statement. Let's take a closer look to understand how revenue works for a very large public company.

Amazon refers to its revenue as "sales," which is equally as common a term. It reports sales in two categories, products and services, which then combine to form total net sales.

In 2017, Amazon recorded $118.6 billion in product sales and $59.3 billion in service sales, for a grand total of $177.9 billion. The figure forms the top line of the income statement.

Beneath that are all operating expenses, which are deducted to arrive at Operating Income, also sometimes referred to as Earnings Before Interest and Taxes (EBIT).

Finally, interest and taxes are deducted to reach the bottom line of the income statement, $3.0 billion of net income.

Revenue Formula

The revenue formula may be simple or complicated, depending on the business. Product sales, is calculated by taking the average price at which goods are sold and multiplying it by the total number of products sold. For service companies, it is calculated as the value of all service contracts, or by the number of customers multiplied by the average price of services.

$$\text{Revenue} = \text{No. of Units Sold} \times \text{Average Price}$$

Or

$$\text{Revenue} = \text{No. of Customers} \times \text{Average Price of Services}$$

The formulae above can be significantly expanded to include more detail. For example, many companies will model their revenue forecast all the way down to the individual product level or individual customer level.

What you should know about Revenue as you begin your startup journey:

- What is the formula for calculating revenue? Also, what are the types of revenue?

- How can we determine the distributional effects of revenue sharing on our startup?

Why are company valuations made based on revenue rather than profit? And how can we determine the valuation of our startup?

What are your forecast projections and their underlying assumptions?

When starting a new business, it's important to have a realistic idea of how profitable it can be. This means creating financial projections - estimating how much revenue your startup can bring in, and what costs you'll incur along the way.

Many factors go into projecting profitability, such as the cost of goods sold, marketing expenses, and labour costs. It's also important to factor in risks, such as the potential for unanticipated costs or a slower-than-expected uptake in sales.

There is no right way to create financial projections, but there are some best practices you can follow. One key step is to make sure your assumptions are realistic. For example, if you're projecting a significant increase in sales, you'll need to have a good reason to believe this will happen.

Overall, financial projections are an important tool for assessing the viability of any new business. They help you make informed decisions about whether to move forward with your startup and give you a realistic idea of what to expect financially. If you're not sure how to create financial projections, there are many resources available online and from your nearest Innovation Hub. With careful planning and realistic assumptions, you can give your startup the best chance for success.

CHAPTER 11

Create sustainable impact.

Define what sustainability and impact mean to you

General definition:

- "A powerful effect that something, especially something new, has on a situation or person."

- "To have an influence on something."

The impact can be negative/adverse, positive/beneficial, catastrophic, or low/high impact!

Types of Impact

- **Economic Impact**: "A financial effect that something, especially something new, has on a situation or person." (i.e., financial inclusion, wealth creation, job creation, gender economic empowerment, inclusive economic growth)

- **Environmental Impact:**   "The effect that activities of people and businesses have on the environment." (i.e., climate change, deforestation, recycling, renewables, eco-friendly products/solutions)

- **Social Impact:** "The net effect of an activity on a community and the well-being of individuals and families." (i.e., health/nutrition, food security, educational outcomes, employment, youth/women's empowerment, art and culture preservation, displacement).

Ensure you are building a sustainable and responsible startup

Operating sustainably is not an option. It is a business imperative. Leaders and business owners are under intense pressure to build sustainable organisations that provide financial value and societal and equitable impact for all stakeholders.

Accenture Future of Work study:

- 65% of employees believe organisations should be responsible for leaving their people "net better off" through work

- 66% of consumers plan to make more sustainable or ethical purchases

- 28% of investors signatories in 2020 to the UN's Principles of Responsible Investment.

Having the voice of the local community and key stakeholders is key for an inclusive economy and business sustainability. Involve the community in the design process: your product, service delivery. They have the solutions.

Key Stakeholders - Your business model should create sustainable value for all your stakeholders:

- Partners and suppliers
- Employees
- Customers
- Communities
- Investors
- Environment

Important to do "Stakeholder Mapping" – to assess the influence and impact of these stakeholders on your business.

Global economic crisis on the back of the COVID-19 pandemic impacted already fragile economies across the world, particularly in Africa.

- Burning issues globally, especially in Africa, include:
- climate change
- poverty
- food insecurity
- vaccine inequity
- educational inequalities

- youth unemployment
- financial and digital exclusion
- labour market skills gaps
- Displacements/refugee/humanitarian crisis

Urgent need for all stakeholders to actively engage in addressing these issues. We now live and work in a very different world and the challenges are intensifying. Businesses will need to take on a large part of the responsibility.

Companies need to transform the way they approach support/impact. There is a need for shared accountability to deliver value and impact for all. The Sustainable Development Goals (SDGs) provide a framework for all stakeholders to contribute to addressing many of the world's challenges.

Decide on your Sustainable Development Goals (SDGs)

The Sustainable Development Goals were set up in 2015 by the United Nations General Assembly.

The 17 SDGs - 17 global goals that should serve as a blueprint to achieve a better and more sustainable future for all by the end of 2030. Which of these are your startup's?

- No Poverty
- Zero Hunger

- Good health and Well-being
- Quality Education
- Gender Equality
- Clean water and Sanitation
- Affordable and Clean Energy
- Decent work and Economic growth
- Industry, Innovation, and Infrastructure
- Reduced Inequalities
- Sustainable Cities and Communities
- Responsible Conduct and Production
- Climate action
- Life below water
- Life on land
- Peace, Justice, and Strong Institutions
- Partnerships for the Goals

Define how you assess, measure, and manage your startup's impact

Key principles of impact measurement:

Measure relative changes compared to the status quo (focus on those areas where you make a change compared to the status quo solution)

- Assess impact from the perspective of stakeholders.

- Reduce complexity with a hypothesis-driven approach.

Impact Indicators are the specific, measurable things that allow businesses to track and assess the effectiveness (the impact) of the planned interventions/ solutions. Setting Key Performance Indicators (KPIs).

Impact Metrics is a defined system or standard of measurement to track the progress of change by your organisation.

Monitoring & Evaluation

Monitoring and evaluation systems must be put in place:

- What to measure
- How to measure
- Whom to measure
- Is the evidence /data telling you that you are making the desired impact?
- Can you quantify the impact you are making?

How to Measure

Traditional data collection and analysis can be expensive and lengthy.

Lean data approach to data collection uses low technology to assess customer/stakeholder needs and to communicate directly with end users.

Lean data approach allows you to collect high-quality data quickly and efficiently.

Your data collection method must give voice to the customer so you can assess the impact/social change.

"The art of every Lean Data approach is in the questions we ask. Ask the wrong questions, and you get back little value. Ask the right ones, and you can move from data to information to actionable insights."

Data Collection

Ways to gather data:

- Focus Groups

- Interviews

- Surveys

- Phone (call centre/researchers, post service calls, etc)

- SMS

- Interactive Voice Response (IVR)

- In person (door to door, face to face)

- Email/online (SurveyMonkey, Qualtrics, Typeform, and Google Forms)

- Data collection is built into your day-to-day operations and activities.

Build your "lean" surveys.

Including for remote, household, customer/ stakeholder surveys.

RULE #1. DRIVE TOWARDS DECISIONS. Before you start to develop a survey, set a goal. What do you want to know? And why?

RULE #2. FOCUS ON YOUR END USER. Make clear WHO you want to take your survey. Who is your target customer? What language will they speak? What might their prior experiences be with surveying and data collection?

RULE #3. MAKE IT RIGOROUS. Even if you're surveying people remotely, the data you collect can still be reliable. Avoid bias.

ESG Sustainability Reporting

What Are Environmental, Social and Governance (ESG) Criteria?

A set of standards for a company's operations that socially conscious investors use to screen potential investments. Environmental criteria consider how a company performs as a steward of nature.

Social criteria examine how it manages relationships with employees, suppliers, customers, and the communities where it operates. Governance deals with a company's leadership, executive pay, audits, internal controls, and shareholder rights.

Annual statutory reports (for example, audited accounts). Annual Sustainability Business Report (aligned to the material, environmental, social, and economic issues identified by your stakeholders).

MILESTONES

To start and sustain a successful technology business in Africa, as in any other continent, a techpreneur requires a compelling vision that will drive the execution of all the activities required to bring it to life as a successful business venture.

The life of that venture is measured by progress towards the realisation of that vision. It is this journey to the successful delivery of the vision by the techpreneur that the innovation hubs and Angel investors seek to join and help along the way with space, time, and money for reward from the expected outcomes in the years to come.

Because Angel investors, innovation hubs and techpreneurs alike are primarily interested in the commercial potential of the venture, the focus must be on how its product/service offer makes money by solving a problem or meeting a need for a specified set of customers and delivers the technology as a product/service offer that satisfies such customers.

Stage 1. Pre-Seed/Incubate Stage

The pre-seed stage of your business life cycle is when your business is just a thought or an idea. This is the very conception or birth of a new business, hence incubation. Most seed-stage companies will have to overcome the challenge of market acceptance and pursue one niche opportunity. Do not spread money and time resources too thinly. At this stage of the business, the focus is on matching the business opportunity with your skills, experience, and passions. Other focal points include: deciding on a business ownership structure, and finding co-founders and professional advisers while planning the business. Early in the business life cycle, with no proven market or customers, the business will rely on cash from the founders, friends, and family. Other potential sources include suppliers, customers, and government grants. The goal of this stage is the creation of a Minimum Viable Product (MVP) that can be put to the addressable target Market.

Stage 2. Seed/Start-Up Stage

At the seed stage, the business has been born and now exists legally. Products or services are in production and you have your first customers. If your business is in the startup life cycle stage, it is likely you have underestimated money needs and the time taken to reach the market. The main challenge is not to burn through what little cash you have. You need to learn what profitable needs your clients have and do a reality check to see if your business is on the right track. Startups require establishing a customer base and market presence, along with tracking and conserving cash flow. The founders, friends, family, Angel investors, suppliers, customers, and grants provide the funding as the business looks for Product-Market Fit (PMF) in an accelerator program with a hub.

Stage 3. Growth Stage

At the growth stage, your business has made it through the toddler stage and is now a child. Revenues and customers are increasing with many new opportunities and issues. Profits are strong, but competition is surfacing. The biggest challenge growth companies face is dealing with the constant range of issues of bidding for more time and money. Effective management is required and a possible new business plan. Learn how to train and delegate to conquer this stage of development. Growth life cycle businesses are focused on running the business in a more formal fashion to deal with the increased sales and customers. Better accounting and management systems will have to be set up. New employees will have to be hired to deal with the influx of business. Banks, profits, grants, partnerships, angels, venture capital, and leasing options become available as the business increasingly acquires repeat customers and breaks even.

Stage 4. Scale Stage

By the time you get to scale, your business has matured into a thriving company with a place in the market and loyal customers. This later stage of the venture's development is characterised by a new period of growth into new markets and distribution channels as the business chooses to gain a larger market share and find new revenue and profit channels. To compete, you will require better business practices, along with automation and outsourcing, to improve productivity. Moving into new markets requires the planning and research of a seed or startup-stage business. The focus should be on businesses that complement your existing experience and capabilities. Moving into unrelated businesses could be disastrous. Add new products or services to existing markets or expand an existing business into new markets and customer types. At this stage, joint ventures, banks, licensing, new investors and partners provide the required funding.

Stage 5. Pre-Exit /Series Stage

This is the big opportunity for your business to cash out on all the effort and years of hard work. Or it can mean shutting down the business. Selling a business requires a realistic valuation. It may have been years of hard work to build the company, but what is its real value in the current marketplace? If you decide to close your business, the challenge is to deal with the financial and psychological aspects of a business loss.

Get a proper valuation of your company. Look at your business operations, management, and competitive barriers to make the company worth more to the buyer. Set up legal buy-sell agreements along with a business transition plan. Find a business valuation partner. Consult with your accountant and financial advisers for the best tax strategy to sell or close down the business.

The POEM Framework ® presents a model that meets the need for organising the business of any company in a form that can be used easily on a day-to-day basis. Each letter in the POEM acronym presents strategic guidance for execution by ensuring critical information is given consideration while leaving its users with the freedom to determine the level of detail required for each activity or peculiar situation, be it operations, marketing, selling, soliciting for funding, recruiting resources, or others.

POEM assessments provide techpreneurs, hubs, investors, and other stakeholders with a tool that can be used with as much documentation as required to give a holistic snapshot of the venture's commercial health at any time.

The best practice I've found is keeping track of the startup's achievements, challenges, and targets for the proposition, organisation, and economics over a rolling two-year horizon. Not too short term, so you can observe trends and not too long term, to the point where assumptions may be too unpredictable, given the African markets.

CHAPTER 12

Be prepared for what's next.

Know where you are on your Startup Journey

As I said at the beginning of this book, to start and sustain a successful technology business in Africa, as in any other place, startup founders require a compelling vision that will drive the execution of all the activities required to bring the vision to life as a successful startup venture. The life of that startup venture is measured by its progress towards the realisation of that vision.

It is that journey to the successful delivery of the vision by the founders that Family, Friends, Fans, Angels, VCs, and others seek to join as early-stage investors and help along the way in exchange for reward from the expected outcomes.

Which POEM Milestones are behind/ahead?

POEM Milestones cover your startup's journey through its funding stages from founder, friends, and family at ideation, angels at growth and VCs at scale to sustainability, recognising that sustainably building startup success follows a curve that dips after launch, known as the Valley of Death, which occurs for several reasons especially:

- Product takes longer than planned to develop

- Customers don't embrace the product as expected

- The business model doesn't work for the market.

Are you at Ideation?

Context

This is where the initial excitement occurs for a startup and the three elements come together: a great idea that solves a significant problem, a strong customer-obsessed team with complementary skills that will support each other during tough times, and money.

This is actually the best time to be raising money because you're selling the dream. When you launch, reality sets in and investors' pockets tighten up.

Key

- Well-defined concept
- Team with a business model
- Expenses funded by the founders, family, friends, and fans (FFFF), grants and competition prizes.

Target

Built Minimum Viable Product (MVP) and have customers.

Are you Pre-Seed?

Context

This is when a startup has released its product to the market and the market provides feedback. It's where the rubber hits the road and reality dawns. It's at this stage that founders really need to listen to their customers to get a reality check and point them in the right direction.

NB: The more time you spend adding features and perfecting your product, the more you fall in love with it, the more rigid your team becomes, and the more difficult it will be to pivot.

Key

- Building out the MVP incrementally

- Learning from the early adopter customer base

- Funding expenses by (FFFF), Grants, Prizes, and Angels

Target

- Established customer base and first external (Angel) funding.

Are you at Seed?

Context

At this stage, the startup needs to make adjustments to its product or business model based on the early adopter customer feedback. There will be several iterations until product market fit is achieved with a growing number of repeat customers, and the startup may have to radically change the product/service offer.

The aim is to iterate the product/service offer through customers' feedback until product-market fit is achieved.

Key

- Establishing the product/service offer to target customers.

- Building an operational structure optimised for delivery.

- Steady burn rate with angel and early-stage VC Funding.

Target

- Product-Market Fit (PMF) and VC Funding.

Are you in Growth?

Context

At this stage, the founders need to optimise the business model making sure that they have a business BEFORE they grow it! This is the stage when the unit economics and business model get figured out to ensure that as the startup grows it makes more money.

The aim is to get to a point where there is a directly demonstrable ROI for any additional funding invested in the startup.

Key

- Increasing customer base and revenues with competitive margins (traction).

- Operations-efficient organisation.

- Repeatable processes independent of individuals.

- Increasing products/service offers that expand revenue base while maintaining existing cost base.

Target

- Product Channel Fit (PCF) using Angel and VC series seed for funding.

Are you Scaling up?

Context

After the business model has been nailed in the growth stage, this is where investment in the startup is able to scale the business. Scaling is characterised by growth from adding new products or services to existing markets or expanding existing business into new markets and customer types, to gain a larger market share and find new revenue and profit channels.

This is when to assemble the best-in-class people, processes, technology, and money necessary to take the company to sustainability.

Key

- Successful growth stage.

- Adding new products or entering new markets.

- Perfecting repeated processes.

- Achieving unit profitability.

Target

- Startup is ready for Series A, B etc. funding from VCs.

Are you Sustainable?

Context

This the stage where the startup graduates to a fully established corporate business. It's about capitalising on the opportunities that have been created by building a strong business and time to reap the benefits of getting through the previous five stages.

At this stage, the startup is reaching maturity and a lot of challenging decisions must be made: should it expand through acquisition or organically, should it take a large buyout offer; should it provide liquidity to investors through a buyback, IPO, or company sale?

Key

- Successful scaling stage.

- Becoming a market leader.

- Valuation that is multiples of where the startup was when scaling.

Target

New corporate vision, trade sale, or if large enough, consider an initial public offering (IPO). POEM Milestones measure your startup's progress throughout this journey by tracking its challenges and achievement of targets on its way through each funding stage. They show where the startup started, where it is today and where it is going as the founders bring their vision to life. Using the POEM framework, they provide an assessment of:

- **Proposition** - how well does the product/ service offer meet customer demand from the market?

- **Organisation** - how well are the people using processes exploiting technology to deliver the proposition?

- **Economics** - how well is the capital being deployed for expenses to generate revenue that's creating impact?

Get investment ready

The process of investment readiness is about preparing answers to some of the essential questions investors will most likely ask of founders as part of their pre-investment due diligence.

Founders should research investors in their ecosystem to understand their strategies and whether their startup is a fit. Investment readiness is essential as it provides the financial and fundraising capability that investors expect from founders, thereby significantly increasing the chances of being funded.

Founders need to prepare before they approach investors to master their options and gain credibility. To do this, founders need to have an up-to-date:

- **Pitch Deck:** a brief presentation that gives potential investors or partners an overview of your business plan, products, services, and growth traction.

- **Business Plan:** a written document that describes in detail how your startup business defines its objectives and how you are to go about achieving its goals.

- **Data Room:** an online cloud storage facility used as a safe place to house important information, such as contracts and corporate documents, so they can be shared securely and confidentially with potential investors.

Have a plausible business plan

A startup business plan is a written document that outlines your ideas and strategies for launching, managing, and eventually exiting your new venture.

It is a living set of documents created from desk and field research, discussions and thinking you have done concerning your startup and the industry segment it will be playing in, showing the current market (as you best understand it through the eyes of those who know), and how you intend to fund and run your startup venture.

Using the POEM framework, your plan should consist of these seven sections:

- Executive Summary
- Vision
- Proposition

- Organisation
- Economics
- Milestones
- References

What's the Executive Summary?

The executive summary is a precis of your business plan and the part of it most read by investors. You write your startup business plan executive summary based on your vision for your startup and how you envision it being brought to life through its operational activities.

Keep it simple and precise. Begin by writing a single sentence startup introduction that showcases the essential customer need/pain point and how your startup solves it. Then summarise the details that can be found in the different sections of the plan, typically writing a paragraph or two for each section of the plan.

What is your vision, mission, and values?

The first step to writing a startup business plan is clarifying your vision of what you want the startup to be. Once you know what your startup does, ask yourself why. What is your startup's mission? What problem will it help customers solve? The startup's vision statement helps define its reason for existing.

It's usually expressed in a simple sentence but can also be written as a short paragraph. Try to answer these questions: What value does your startup create? How will it make money? How quickly do you expect it to grow? Are there any significant events or deadlines ahead that need to be met?

What's your startup's proposition?

Your startup's proposition is what will define your venture and distinguish you from your competitors. Writing your proposition is a great way to visualise, design and test how you can create value for your customers in the market. It's what should excite your customers to do business with you and will play a significant role in determining if they will choose your startup's product or service instead of your competitors.

Note: even an exceptional proposition can still fail if your business model is flawed, or your customer knowledge is not accurate, appropriate, relevant, or up to date.

This section of your business plan and pitch deck should include:

- The Problem/Opportunity
- The Solution
- The Market, Regulation, Competition
- The Customers

- The Business Idea, Model
- The Products & Services.

How's your startup organised?

Founders tend to be and should be the primary owners of their startup with Board seats. Most startups adopt a flat organisational structure in the early years, which gives them a good result. Startups, however, grow faster than mature ventures but some keep the structure the same. This can slow the rapid growth of the venture and can even put a stop to it.

The right organisation to keep the success sustainable must be based on the stage that the startup has reached, as in each stage, it will need a different organisation.

This section of your business plan and pitch deck should include:

- The Ownership
- The Governance
- The Executive, Management, Employees
- The Organisation, Ecosystem, Partners
- The Strategy, Plan, Process, Procedures
- The Marketing, Sales, and Distribution
- The Operations, Logistics
- The Technology, Security

What is your startup economics?

When planned carefully, your startup's economics can set it up for success. You should be aiming to carry out this analysis as soon as you are confident of your startup vision and co-founder selections, or at the very latest, before raising external funding.

Many startup founders prefer to focus on building a great venture first and then figuring out the economics over time, which could be even more time and money wasted if you don't get it right at the start. Attention to the economic aspects of startups tends to focus on the external measure of fundraising.

Yet before this, there are many aspects for founders to consider while setting up their startup for economic success.

This section of your business plan and pitch deck should include:

- The Capital Funding and Finance
- The Customer Economics
- The Revenue Model
- The Cost Profile
- The Financial Projections
- The Risks and Mitigations
- The Social Impact and Measurements

What are your startup's milestones?

Right from the beginning, founders need to identify the most important events or actions that must occur to bring their vision to life. Some events are prerequisites to others and you need to develop a critical-path milestone chart that displays their sequence.

Identify the significant assumptions on which the startup venture's success depends and how milestones will test each assumption. As each event occurs and replaces assumptions with information, review the planned future milestones, adjusting as required.

Evaluate performance based on what you have learned and what you can apply, and design your financing, resource allocations and rewards based on the results achieved.

This section of your business plan and pitch deck should include:

- The Achievements
- The Challenges
- The Current Status
- The Assumptions
- The Future Milestones

What are your references?

For your pitch deck and business plan to secure funding for your startup, you must cite your sources. Your plan will have topics and statistics covering your target market, population demographics, spending habits, market trends, market growth etc. Investors know how to double check assumptions and will have no qualms about calling your bluff and stopping the funding if they don't believe your stats.

If you forecast increasing revenue, you'd better be able to document how a similar product or service did the same, and why yours will follow suit, and not crash and burn in a saturated niche market. So do your research and develop your forecasts using that information, making sure you document your sources in references.

This section of your business plan and pitch deck should include:

- The Analysis
- The Plans
- The Forecasts
- The Surveys
- The Reports
- The Other Documents

How do you pitch it to Investors?

- Keep your pitch simple and manage timing.
- Tell your story and stay focused.
- Convey the unique value of your product or service.

- Let investors experience your product first-hand.

- Be clear on who your target customer is and why.

- Know your numbers and be prepared to support any claims.

- Be passionate and enthusiastic about the opportunity.

- Present a solid pitch deck with a strong close.

- Build a strong support team to market your social value.

- Dress professionally and practice, practice, practice.

What comes after the pitch?

If the investors like what they hear in the pitch, they will usually ask to meet the founder to get more information. If the startup venture and team match their investment thesis and risk profile, they will typically issue a Term Sheet, which outlines the material terms and conditions by which the investor will invest in the startup.

It acts as a template that, when agreed upon by both parties, is used as a reference point to develop a detailed set of legally binding documents. In early-stage investing, term sheets are given to successful candidates by a Lead Investor once a Syndicate, Network or Fund has agreed to begin the investment process and due diligence.

The idea is that once the term sheet is agreed and signed, the only scenario whereby an investment would not occur is if the founders have misrepresented the startup venture and this is uncovered in due diligence.

Are you ready for Due Diligence?

Due Diligence is an investigation of the startup company for possible investment by an investor. The first funding rounds for startups are often by Angel investors who invest their own money and view risk differently from venture capitalists.

Venture capitalists perform full due diligence of the operating business, whereas Angel investors undertake soft due diligence to see if the startup venture and team match their investment-risk comfort level.

Typical check points for soft due diligence:

People: Getting to know the founders and team, their capabilities and commitment!

Market: Understanding who the competitors are, and what edge is needed to succeed in the market.

IP Rights: Do they have full control over IP, code, logos, and relevant domains?

Code review: Is the code well written, and is the platform scalable?

Budget & forecasts: Are they in control of the finances?

Traction: Investigate actual revenue growth, user growth, retention, churn, etc.

Online profile: What image do they convey e.g. do they attract followers on social media?

Contracts: Check the essential key customer / employee / vendor contracts!

Topics you can expect to discuss with your Investors...

- Competition
- Comparatives
- Unit Economics
- Breakeven
- CAC/CLV
- MoM Growth
- Mentoring
- Advisory
- Equity
- Debt
- Valuations
- Exit

APPENDIX 1

Questions you can expect from Investors

1. What problem (or need) are you solving?

2. What kinds of people, groups, or organisations have that problem? How many are there, where are they, what are they doing about it now?

3. How are you different?

4. Who will you compete with? How are they different?

5. How will you make money?

6. How will you make money for your investors?

7. How fast can you grow your business? Can you scale up volume without proportionally scaling up headcount?

8. What's proprietary? What are you going to do to defend that?

9. What traction have you made?

10. What milestones have you met?

11. How are you going to get the word out?

12. How are you going to close sales?

13. How are you going to get started?

14. How are you going to spend investors' money?

15. What makes your team suited for this business?

16. How did you come up with this idea?

17. Why did you decide to (some marketing, product, or financial decision in the pitch)?

18. What about (some objections related to market, competition, financial plans)?

19. Who are your investors so far?

20. How strong is your patent?

21. Could you grow faster with more money?

22. Do you realise you're vastly underestimating your marketing expenses (or sales expense, or margins through channels, or headcount required for direct selling)?

23. Do you know comparable numbers for similar businesses?

24. Why don't you do this yourself? (Meaning, why do you think you need investors?)

25. What sales have you made so far?

26. Have you actually talked to those companies?

27. Who else is interested?

28. Who else have you shown this to?

29. How did you come up with that valuation?

30. Why would anybody want this?

31. What is your burn rate per month?

32. What is your traction?

33. When will you start making money?

34. When will you break even?

Made in the USA
Columbia, SC
26 July 2024

39406150R00115